Leadership Development

How to Think and Communicate as a Leader

John Mitchell

Published by:
Mitchell Leadership Consulting,
Grand-Rue 84
1820 Montreux
Switzerland

ISBN 10: 1481151215
ISBN 13: 9781481151214

To order additional copies, please email your request to:
contact@mitchell-lc.com

Contents

A Leader is best
When people barely know he exists,
Not so good when people obey and acclaim him,
Worst when they despise him.

Fail to honor people -
They fail to honor you:

But of a good Leader, who talks little,
When his work is done, his aim fulfilled,
They will all say:

"We did this ourselves."

(Lao Tzu)

CHAPTER 1

The Language of Leadership Development

A story set in medieval times tells of a traveller who comes upon three stone-masons. He asks each in turn: 'What are you doing?'

The first answers, without hesitation: 'I am cutting this stone.' The second, who appears to the traveller to be doing an identical job, makes a gesture with his hand and says: 'I am completing the wall.' The third, who again seems to be engaged in the same activity, slowly raises his eyes to the sky and quietly affirms: 'I am building a cathedral.'

For the present-day business leader, whether actual or aspiring, the story offers a useful analogy, because it brings into question the nature of the relationship between awareness and activity or, in the language we shall develop, between vision and action.

The quality of vision determines the quality of action. And with this simple analogy, we can already begin to see that the quality of vision may vary without visible change in the quality of action.

This relationship is important for everyone interested in the quality of performance and, ultimately, in the quality of life.

The big picture and the detail

Let's study, for a moment, the situation of the second stone-mason - the one who is focused on completing a wall. What will determine the quality of his work? First, there is a skill requirement, a level of basic ability. The mason must be able to construct a wall that will stand and fulfill its essential supporting, separating or decorative function. This involves the right depth of foundation, adequate materials and tools and the knowledge of how to use them effectively.

Second, there is an attitude requirement. Ability on its own is no guarantee of quality or effectiveness. If the mason is impatient, is easily distracted, is careless, or has developed an uncontrollable dislike of the local bishop, the end product may be flawed or incomplete.

Assuming that ability and attitude are already strong, what further ingredient will influence the quality of action, and therefore of result? We come to the question of vision. From an awareness of his physical activity in relation to the wall, the mason's vision can be stretched to include more of the bigger picture and more of the detail. In this case, the bigger picture will focus on the relationship of the wall to the cathedral, while the detail may include, for example, greater attention to the exactness of each cut.

The sources of quality

A few hours, or days, invested in concentrating on the role of the wall in the context of the great edifice of the cathedral may result in a variety of modifications. Perhaps there will be adjustments for the benefit of harmony with the wall opposite. Perhaps a new question will be raised about the design of a window - a question that would not otherwise have emerged until much later. Perhaps an element of design, attractive in itself, will be found to be inappropriate in the larger context.

Similarly, greater attention to detail may result in decisions, that would not otherwise be made, having an impact on overall quality. Greater precision in the pointing, or in the exact coloration of the stone, may have a significant effect on the perceptions of future pilgrims - an aspect the mason may normally be quite unaware of yet which, he now remembers being told, formed the central focus of the original conception of the cathedral.

Perhaps, more significantly still, the very act of stretching awareness to include, in one direction, the overall view and, in the other direction, greater detail, may have a consequent effect on the mason's attitude. This in turn may inspire him to identify and develop further refinements of his ability. It may even have a more subtle effect on them, which he might not notice and could not explain.

Disharmony between vision and action

The successful construction of anything we make, from a cathedral or a house to a meal or a business, requires a correspondence and harmony between vision and action. In constructing a building, the actions of those working on the site must correspond to the implications of the architect's plans. Similarly, the ingredients and cooking times used by a chef must correspond to the requirements of the eventual meal. In both cases there may be additional criteria to be met, based on the expectations of those who will use the building or eat the meal.

The same principles apply in business, government and other organizations. Yet often there is disharmony between vision and action. The vision, expressed in terms of a corporate plan or direction, may come from one person or group, while others have the responsibility for its implementation. This recipe for disharmony was characteristic of much corporate strategy in the last 20 years, often sowing the seeds of failed or unacceptably painful mergers and acquisitions.

Alternatively, a board or senior management team may wish, or be expected, to act in harmony without first establishing a shared vision. Here is another recipe for discomfort and waste, featuring ineffectual debates, stalemates and demotivation.

While disharmony can exist at corporate and team levels, it may also exist at a personal level. The actions of individuals, whether they realize it or not, may be out of line with their own vision. Often this, too, becomes a recipe for stress and conflict.

The challenge for leaders

In today's environment of rapid change and international expansion, finding ways of harmonizing vision and action at corporate, team and personal levels can be seen as the greatest leadership challenge; and meeting this challenge will give any organization a competitive advantage through the higher standards of morale, and the quality and speed of making and implementing decisions that will become possible.

This book is intended, at least in part, as a guide for the creation of such competitive advantage. Like our stone-mason, tomorrow's manager needs to see more of the bigger picture and more of the detail. Life, it seems, was slower in the middle ages: the cathedral might take a generation to build, providing a constant focus. In the type of building that managers are erecting in today's business equivalent, the walls are constantly changing! And all around, other managers are building walls in different styles - and the quality of stone is so unreliable!

An expansion of vision is the key to every aspect of quality, and to generate that, we need tools. Where the mason uses bricks and mortar, we shall use experience and ideas. Where the mason uses a chisel, we shall use language - which confronts us with a major difficulty.

Criteria for leadership terminology

The language of business and management contains a mixture of everyday terms and jargon. This has a double disadvantage. First, the everyday words commonly used in business, such as plan, idea, authority, communication and management, lack clear definition.

To take just one example, the word 'strategy' is widely used as an alternative for any of the following words: plan, idea, intention, objective, policy, wish and - perhaps most frequently - tactics.

Second, jargon such as 'empowerment', 'process re-engineering' and 'total quality management' creates the illusion (and often the reality!) of a quite unnecessary complexity.

The first part of our challenge, then, will be to agree on a group of clearly defined terms with which we can explore the relationship between vision and action. Since our intended direction is towards simplicity rather than added complexity, we shall utilize words already in current use, rather than create more jargon. This means reaching, first, a new quality of definition of key terms.

If we are to develop a language that will be of practical use in strategic decision-making, particular characteristics are needed in the definition of key terms. These may differ considerably from those prevalent in conventional textbooks. A practicing business manager might struggle, for instance, to find very much of practical use in the following definition of strategy, proposed by James Brian Quinn, the William and Josephine Buchanan Professor of Management at Dartmouth University: *Strategy 'is the pattern or plan that integrates an organization's major goals, policies and action sequences into a cohesive whole.' Well formulated, it 'helps to marshal and allocate an organization's resources into a unique and viable posture based upon its relative internal competences and shortcomings, anticipated changes in the environment, and contingent moves by intelligent opponents.'*

As good definitions should, it searches for universality. Its limitation may be that it only describes, and does not define. It is rather like trying to define a meal merely by describing its appearance on the table.

Our definitions will aim for universality, with an important central difference. They will also aim to expose relationships which can contribute to the growth of vision. In leadership, we need to know what something is in terms of the part it plays in a bigger scenario - i.e. how it is related to its environment.

This is the purpose that our terminology must serve.

Our agenda for definitions

We shall begin with definitions of terms we have already started to use: vision, action, attitude and ability. Then we shall need to define other key terms central to our theme: decision, decision-making, management and leadership. These in turn will require consistent and precise definitions of two elusive ingredients: authority and responsibility. We shall then define strategy, and prepare for a deeper exploration in Chapters 2 and 4 of the specific meanings and interrelationships of its key components: purpose, aim, objective and tactic.

As we progress, we shall examine the place and role of thinking, of meetings and of culture in relation to management decision-making. By the end of this first chapter, these main elements of our language will be in place, and we shall have our essential terminology for leadership development.

Vision = Knowledge of relatedness

We shall define vision as knowledge of relatedness. As is already implied in the analogy of the stone-mason, an expansion of practical knowledge about how things or ideas are related to each other can result in new decisions and higher quality results.

To take a global example, towards the end of the last century there was an expansion of knowledge concerning our impact on the earth and its atmosphere. This led to a shift of attitude, resulting in the passing and implementing of new laws and, in many businesses, the generation of new policies and procedures. While the decision-making entailed was not strategic in the full sense implied in this book, the example illustrates the central importance of vision in all decision-making.

This definition is related to, and yet quite different from, two conventional uses of the word vision. One is the meaning of dream or apparition. The second is the meaning of a visualized goal or expectation.

In Chapters 2 and 3 we shall see more clearly that these uses may represent different degrees of understanding characteristic of different levels or, as we shall call them, levels of leadership awareness and performance.

Attitude = Emotional posture

Just as we have a physical posture, we have also an emotional posture, and this will be our definition of attitude. And as with the stone-mason, our own attitude - evidenced, for example, in our level of openness, receptivity, willingness, feeling of well-being - is heavily influenced by our vision, our knowledge of relatedness.

The part needs to know how it is related to the whole. This is as true of a child in a family or at school as it is of an adult at work or a whole organization in its particular environment. When organizations no longer know how they are related to their environment, they will always pay the price in terms of morale and confidence and, consequently, in effectiveness and enjoyment.

Not only individuals, but also groups of people and whole organizations have an attitude - a recognizable flavor which, in the case of businesses, can often be sensed before one even sets foot in the building.

Ability = Facility of execution

Being good at something means we find it relatively easy to do well. How do we acquire this ability? Leaving aside, for the moment, the question of genius or exceptional talent, we can identify fundamental steps in the development of ability. These are of great importance to the strategic decision-maker, who will by definition be interested in developing the abilities related to decision-making.

A mother sends her 8-year-old daughter for her first piano lesson. Both are apprehensive. The mother remembers her own false start - a series of battles with `5-finger exercises' that were forced on her and soon killed any interest or ability she might have had. The daughter, sensing her mother's anxiety, is nervous of meeting the teacher and of what the whole experience might be like.

Early in the lesson the teacher asks the girl what tunes she likes. She remembers her favorite song. The teacher asks if she would like to be able to play it. The girl says yes. In a few minutes, she can play the melody of the first line. Surprised at how easy it is, she continues, and practices when she gets home.

Some time later, a new piece is needed. The teacher asks the child what music she would like to learn, and plays a selection.

The girl chooses. They start work, and the teacher explains how certain exercises will help improve her technique. She works on these, and makes her own decision to learn some 5-finger exercises.

Soon, she's entertaining her friends with their favorite songs.

Manipulation

Manipulation is an attempt to alter others' actions without fostering the growth of their vision. Motivation comes from a growth of vision. We can visualize the relationship between vision, attitude and ability as concentric rings, with vision at the centre and ability at the perimeter. A change in vision can have a ripple effect on attitude and, consequently, on ability, rather like a stone dropped into a pond. To become expert in strategic decision-making, we need to expand our understanding of the relationships implicit in Figure 1.1, between vision (knowledge of relatedness), attitude (emotional posture) and ability (facility of execution).

After all, decision-making is hardly a new subject - we have been making decisions since early childhood! The challenge is to bring a fresh, questioning attitude so that we can see much more about this central aspect of our existence, and define new possibilities.

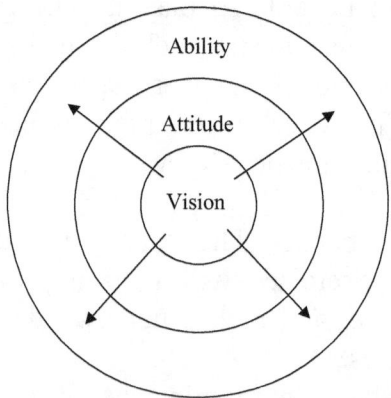

Figure 1.1 Vision, attitude and ability

In this spirit of exploration, we shall investigate the fundamental nature and relationship of management and leadership.

The difference between management and leadership

What is management? When practicing managers are asked this question, the definitions they give invariably describe some aspect of the manager's own actions, tasks or intentions. Examples abound in books on management: 'getting results through others', 'achieving profit targets', 'planning and implementing strategy', 'making it happen', and so on.

We shall define management as the conduct of the relationship between responsibility and authority. This gives a definition in which all managers can recognize their own activity, and at the same time it raises new questions. What is the nature of the relationship between responsibility and authority? How is this relationship connected with the daily performance of practicing managers? Who or what is a manager?

Taking this last question first, we can note that the title of manager is conventionally used for those who are given authority to control the use of a resource, which may or may not be their own. We are most familiar with the application of this term in business. Yet, in a wider sense, who is not a manager?

We all have the possibility of exerting at least some degree of control or influence over resources that may or may not belong to us. These include, and are by no means restricted to, our abilities, our time, other people (employees, kids, friends, colleagues), other people's property, the house we live in, the car we drive, and so on. Through the decisions we make in relation

15

to all these resources, we inevitably exert an influence. In this wider sense, like the stone-mason, we are all managers in that we all have the possibility of conducting a relationship between authority and responsibility.

Authority and responsibility

Since the words authority and responsibility have entered our definition of management, and since they are generally used inconsistently, we shall also create definitions for them.

By authority we shall mean the external limitations on decision-making. These come from the context within which the manager operates. They include limits set both from within the organization, generally through interaction with a superior, and from outside, in the form of codes of practice and rules and regulations.

These may be restricted to specific areas of activity or encompass local, national and international law.

By responsibility we shall mean the internal limitations on decision-making. These are the limitations on decision-making that come from the manager's own thinking, attitude and vision.

They determine, quite literally, the manager's ability to respond within the context created through authority.

What is this context? It is a remarkable yet rarely observed fact that the vast majority of managers operate within structural contexts which, from the point of view of relationship, are identical. While those with management roles within professional practices, partnerships and 'non-hierarchical' structures may often appear not to operate within such a context, close scrutiny of the subtleties of operation within such

16

organizations generally reveals that, in reality, they do.

The context of management and leadership

The context within which managers and leaders operate is almost universally a structure of four primary relationships based on authority. These four relationships are illustrated in Figure 1.2. The fundamental relationship is 'upwards' - the relationship with a person or persons with a higher level of authority. This is the fundamental relationship because the other three depend on it.

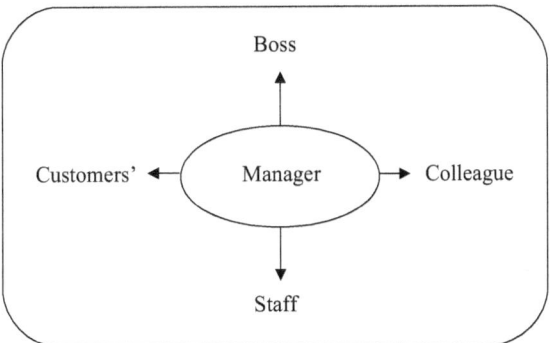

Figure 1.2 The context of management

If, for example, the "upward" relationship is terminated, then the other relationships are also terminated - at least in their existing form. In business life, this is the relationship with the "boss". For a chief executive, it may be the relationship with the board or shareholders. For an entrepreneur starting a new business, it may be the relationship with the bank manager.

The "downward" relationship is the relationship with those

at a lower level of authority, and for whom the manager is 'boss'. They are his or her 'direct reports', accountable to the manager for the quality of their performance.

The two remaining relationships are 'sideways', that is, they are with groups of people with a broadly equivalent level of authority.

One of these, the peer group, is the group of close colleagues who report to the same senior manager. The other is the wider group of those in other parts of the organization, or in other organizations, who have a broadly equivalent level of authority. These may include customer and supplier contacts though, as we shall see, these relationships may be more mobile, in terms of differences in authority, than those within the organization.

The context of management is the framework of personal relationships that derive from the existence of a position of authority, executed with a greater or lesser feeling of responsibility.

The relationship between authority and responsibility will occupy us throughout the book. Let us now focus on the activities through which they become visible.

The activities of management

We have defined the nature of management, and the context in which it operates. Then how does it operate? What are the activities through which these four primary relationships are brought to life, and through which the relationship between authority and responsibility is therefore conducted?

If we are to believe a great deal of discussion and published material on management, we are informed that management is a hugely complex affair, that managers have all kinds of complicated activities to perform and, if you are a manager, that there are a million and one things to do and `get right'. From the point of view of strategic decision-making, this apparent complexity is an illusion. In reality, there are only two activities in management: thinking and communicating (see Figure 1.3). When both are of high quality, management becomes relatively simple.

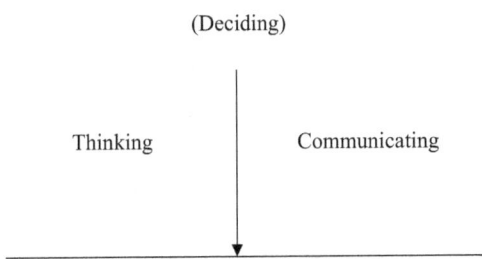

Figure 1.3 The activities of a manager

While it may seem that decision-making is also an activity, the split second in which a decision is made occupies such a tiny span of time that it can hardly be counted. All activities specific to management are included in thinking and communicating.

Creating plans, pondering, digesting new information and absorbing new ideas are all part of thinking. Speaking, listening, writing letters and memos, advertising and participating in meetings are all part of communication. Apart from thinking and communicating, all other activities undertaken by managers are supportive of their role without being an essential part of it.

These include driving cars, eating, drinking, using computers and so on.

Yet each of these activities actually provides opportunities for management, as defined above, on different levels. We can even say that, at a higher level of strategic thinking, using machines and the care of one's own physique both form part of communication.

What is Leadership?

Leadership, like management, is the conduct of the relationship between authority and responsibility. The context is the same, and the activities are the same. Leaders operate within the same fundamental set of relationships as managers, and they have two activities, thinking and communicating. So what's the difference?

The difference between leadership and management is a difference in attitude towards the conduct of the four primary relationships, which give the context. Put very simply, management is relatively passive and leadership is relatively active in the conduct of these relationships.

The transformation from manager to leader needs mainly a development in attitude, which can come from an expansion of vision. The difference will be experienced in the quality of decision-making.

A new definition of 'decision'

What are decisions? They are constantly 'made' in both private and business life. Yet it can be hard to elicit from practicing managers or from published material a consistent view of what decisions are. We shall define a decision as the moment of transition from internal to external action (Figure 1.4).

This definition will be useful in a number of ways. First, it gives protection from the mistake of imagining that a decision can exist in isolation or is independent from the actions that precede and follow it.

In strategic decision-making, a decision exists only when the action(s) implicit in it are taken within the stated or implied time period. If this does not happen, then another decision has in reality

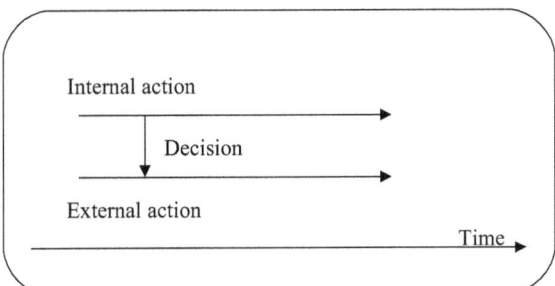

Figure 1.4 Decision = Moment of transition.

been taken - a decision not to change. This decision then supersedes the first 'decision', which is thus revealed to have been an ineffectual statement of intent - not a decision.

Second, this definition provides interesting possibilities for determining differences between various types of decision, by articulating differences between the levels of 'internal action' that precede it. We shall explore these in Chapter 2, and also find ways to be more exact about what constitutes quality in decision-making.

Internal and external action

A third benefit of our definition of decision - as the moment of transition from internal to external action - is that it will give the possibility for creative links to be perceived between decision-making by an individual, by a group and by an organization. For these to emerge, we shall first need to investigate and define the meaning of internal and external action.

We shall define action as the expenditure of energy: internal action is invisible; external action is visible. Individuals, teams and whole organizations all have internal and external actions. The internal action of organizations is made up of the external action of groups. The internal action of groups is made up of the external action of individuals.

We have already seen that, in the case of individuals, decision-making comes between the activities of thinking and communicating. Thinking is the internal, invisible action of individuals.

While communication is ideally the external action, we know that communication does not always happen when it is attempted! So we shall define external action, in terms of an individual, as personal influence.

The four components of decision-making

We have now identified three components of the decision-making process: internal action, decision and external action. They occur in that order. The quality of external action will depend on the quality of decision. This will in turn depend on the quality of internal action. But what determines the quality of internal action?

Here we come to the key ingredient, which will determine the parameters of the quality of internal action and, consequently, of the whole process. The fourth component is defined as the moment of transition from external to internal action. In the case of decision-making by an individual, this will take the form of a question.

These four components give an outline of the process of decision-making in an individual, a group of people or a whole organization (see Figure 1.5).

Decision-making by individuals

Working from this outline, we can now translate the four components into a more specific definition of the process relating to individuals, groups and organizations.

In the case of an individual, we have defined internal action as thought and external action as personal influence. The moment of transition between personal influence and thought, which influences the quality of the decision, is created by a question.

Leadership Development

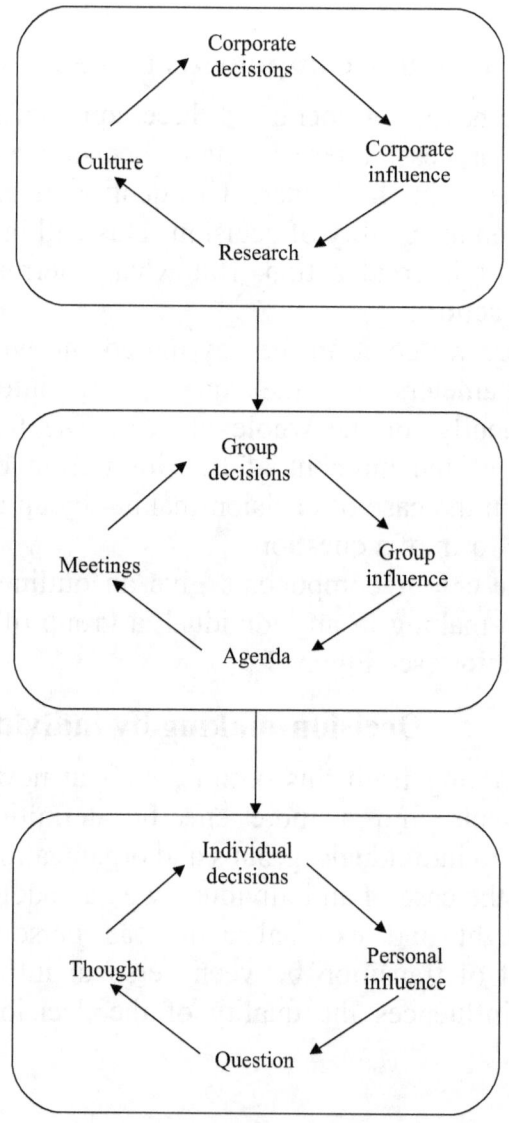

Figure 1.5 Decision-making by individuals, by groups and by organizations.

Decision-making by groups

What are the aspects of group activity that correspond to an individual's thinking and personal influence? It is clear that, within a group, the elements, which interact are the group members, through their mutual personal influence. Such interaction may take many forms: discussions, formal and informal, telephone calls, memos and all kinds of subtler messages which, consciously or not, form part of the combined personal influences of the group members.

In the same way as we applied the term thinking to represent the internal action of a person, we shall use the word meetings to indicate the totality of activities which constitute the interaction between members of a group. This internal action is invisible to those who are not in the group. And just as we have used the term personal influence for the external action of an individual, so we shall use the term group influence to indicate the outer action of a group. This may be a combined representative influence exerted by all or some members of the group, as in an orchestra, or the totality of influences of individual members acting separately.

Substituting the terms meetings and group influence for internal and external action in the original definition, we can therefore define a group decision as the moment of transition between meetings and group influence.

To complete the cycle of decision-making by groups, we need to find the equivalent term in relation to meetings to the role played by a question in relation to individual thought. It is the *agenda* which provide the corresponding determinant of quality in meetings and, consequently, in the quality of group decisions and influence.

Decision-making by organizations

The internal action of the whole organization is the sum of the internal action of the individuals and groups within it: the totality of thought and meetings. In the language of strategic decision-making, this totality is the definition of corporate culture. The external action of the whole organization is the corporate influence within its environment. This gives a definition of corporate decisions as moments of transition between corporate culture and corporate influence.

What then is the moment of transition between corporate influence and corporate culture? For an organization, this point in the decision cycle - which corresponds to the place occupied by a question for individuals and by agenda for groups - is filled by *research*.

Does an organization really make decisions?

The idea that an organization, rather than an individual or group representing it, can make a decision, may at first seem strange. We are used to the notion that a chief executive or board, for example, can make decisions on behalf of the whole organization. But in the language we are developing, these are individual (the chief executive) or group (the board) decisions, made in accordance with authority.

To see the reality of corporate decisions, we have to picture the organization as a whole in motion within its environment. It moves in a certain way, with a greater or lesser degree of consistency. Corporate decisions and influence concern the points of contact with the environment. Some of these, such as annual reports and advertising, are obvious. Other are less obvious. We shall call the totality of these points of contact, whether obvious or not, corporate influence.

It is the corporate influence - the influence exerted by the organization as a whole - which forms the external action resulting from corporate decisions. If an organization has 1000 employees, then there are perhaps 10,000 to 20,000 elements of corporate influence every day. Every telephone call, letter or other element of communication made on behalf of the organization is an element of the organization's external action.

Generally speaking, the myriads of corporate decisions that result in corporate influence are not consciously made. We shall see more about their level - in terms of the quality of decision-making - in Chapter 2. For now, we may note that initiatives to raise the corporate awareness of customers and to enhance customer service are related to the question of the quality of corporate decisions and influence. The qualitative relationship between individual, group and corporate decision-making is illustrated in Figure 1.5.

Strategy and its components

We have defined decision, vision, action, attitude, ability, management, leadership, authority and responsibility. What of strategy?

Strategy is the conscious translation of vision into action. This means both internal and external action, and we shall define its components as follows:

1. Vision	Knowledge of relatedness
2. Purpose (or mission)	The contribution of a lower authority in respect of a higher authority
3. Strategic aims	Signposts for action to fulfill purpose
4. Objectives	Concrete measures of productivity in relation to aim
5. Tactics	The application of resources towards aims and objectives.

The internal action, which forms part of strategy, is the formulation of purpose, aim and objectives and tactics. The external action is the influence exerted through communication and attempts at communication.

In the following chapters, we shall continue to build our language of strategic decision-making through creating and exploring further definitions of these components of strategy.

Three overlapping layers of strategic awareness

A central theme of the book will be the need for the development of at least three layers of strategic awareness. This will apply to the growth of individuals, groups and organizations alike (see Figure 1.6).

For an individual, the layers may be related as follows. The first level will be an awareness of some parts of the strategy of the context. This may mean, for example, the aims and objectives of an immediate superior.

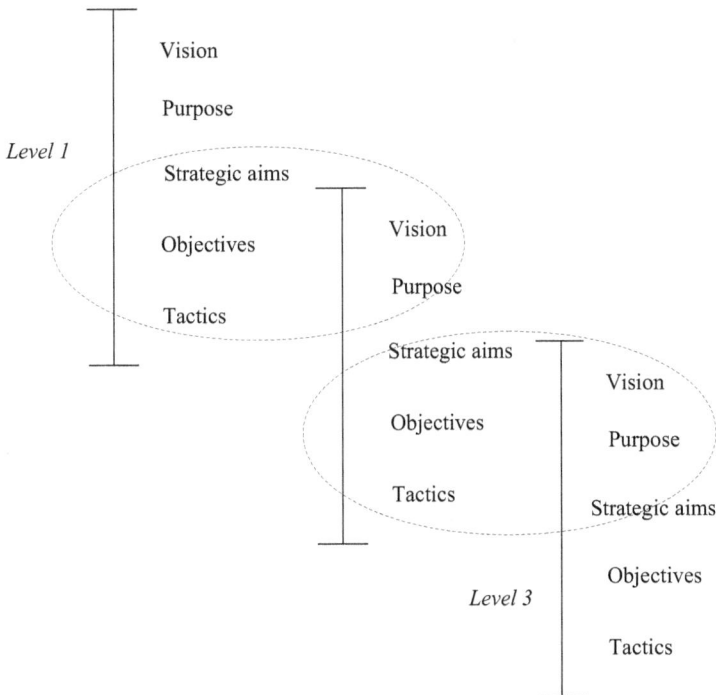

Figure 1.6 Three overlapping layers of strategic awareness

The second layer may be the individual's personal strategy, articulated in the form of the strategic role definition discussed in Chapter 3. The third layer may be the strategy for the management of a particular relationship.

The strategic decision-maker, as defined in this book, is aware on these three levels. The service-oriented organization, made up of strategic decision-makers, also has these three layers of awareness - both internally and in relation to its environment.

Language for leadership development

In this chapter we have articulated the key terms and concepts that will make possible both the discussion and the practice of leadership development.

We have also established that management and leadership denote complementary attitudes to the conduct of the relationship between authority and responsibility. At the centre of all management and leadership capability, determining the precise nature of these attitudes, is the degree of vision, which we have defined as knowledge of relatedness.

We need a fresh idea of what constitutes a leader, and to define this we shall need to see more clearly how the degree of vision is related to different degrees, or levels, of leadership.

CHAPTER 2

Three Levels of Leadership

Quality in decision-making

We have defined decision as the moment of transition between internal and external action. In opening up the subject of decision-making, we have explored the four elements of the process and how these are adapted to individuals, groups and organizations. Now we shall investigate in more detail the question of what constitutes quality in decision-making - irrespective of who is making the decision, or how many people are involved.

What makes a good decision? To explore this, we can draw on our own experience. What decisions, for example, can you remember making in the last 24 hours? (It may be interesting to spend a few minutes creating a list of, say, 10 decisions made in that time.) To catch a certain bus or train? To accept or refuse a discount? To drink a cup of coffee? If you do make a list, it can also be useful to note down how many options you were aware of in reaching each decision.

Closed decisions

Unpublished research conducted between 2000 and 2010, which included data from hundreds of company executives around the world, indicates strongly that the vast majority of decisions which most executives remember making are the result of a perceived choice between two alternatives. In most instances, the thought process that led to the decision took the form of a 'closed' question, that is, a question that will allow only two possible answers: 'yes' or 'no', 'this' or 'that'. It may be that your own examples follow this pattern - or are you an exception?

We shall label this type of decision - where a choice is perceived between a limited number of predefined courses of action - a *closed* decision. Closed decisions range from responses to simple yes/no questions to the multiple-choice formats familiar in certain types of questionnaire, such as psychometric tests.

Automatic decisions

As soon as we become aware of the preponderance of closed decisions in everyday activity, we are then in a position to detect the existence of a second type of decision which also plays a significant part in daily life. What about all the activities that unquestionably take place and for which we do not remember making a decision? Turning left or right out of the road we live in; lifting the telephone; taking a sip of tea. The more we look dispassionately at what happens, the more we can see that unconscious habit plays an extremely important part in our decision-making and relieves us of the necessity to make separate closed decisions for a great deal of our activity.

As these decisions are invisible and lie behind our most habitual activities, we shall call them *automatic* decisions. They differ from closed decisions by the fact that no alternative line of action is perceived.

Open decisions

What do you consider to be the best decision you have ever made?

Again, it may be worth taking a few minutes to think this through and to note down your personal response. Based on the research already mentioned, most people find that the decision they consider to have been particularly good was not necessarily made recently, may have involved a lengthy period of reflection and even confusion, may have involved what appeared to be a risk, and may have brought about - or prevented - a significant change. It may also have been influential in determining environmental or operating conditions for the decision-maker and/or other people over a relatively extended period of time.

What was the nature of the thought processes that led to the making of such a decision? In the research referred to above, it was found that, while a final choice may have existed which was resolved into a closed question, this was generated outside of the pressure of immediate circumstances in response to a wider, more open question. An open question is one that contains no trace of a preconceived answer; the situation is experienced as new.

We shall call such decisions *open*. While they may ultimately become a question of, for example, whether or not to join/leave a certain company or to begin/end a relationship (and the 'best' decisions of many managers are about their relationships), open decisions - in the context of individuals - have certain features in common: they result from, and contribute to, an expansion of vision and, in so doing, create new possibilities of personal influence.

Quality of decision is related to quality of question

So far, we have discerned three quite different levels of decision-making: automatic, closed and open. These are distinguished by contrasting levels of thinking, of attitude and of vision. These levels are reflected in the type of question that generates the internal action leading to the decision.

At the lowest level of awareness are the automatic decisions which come about as a result of ingrained habit or reflex - that is to say, the actions to which they are a response do not enter our awareness. In effect, there is no question.

At the next level are what we have called closed decisions. Here a perceived choice exists between two or more options, and the decision is reached in response to a closed question, i.e. one that generates a yes/no answer or a response to the question 'Which . . .?'

We have also identified a third level - open decisions - which generate new possibilities for future closed and automatic decisions through a response to open questions - questions which embody a recognition of the newness of a situation and carry the genuine nature of enquiry implicit in the interrogative pronouns. (In the English language, the main ones are: why . . .?, what . . .?, who . . .?, how . . .?, when . . .? and where . . .? However, it should be noted that a question formulated as an open question can actually have the meaning and effect of a closed question, while it is also possible for a particularly attentive listener to detect an underlying open question behind a question formulated as closed.) To define and understand the fourth level, strategic decision-making, we need first to see more clearly how these first three are related to the practice of management and leadership.

To establish this perspective, we will explore three bandwidths of decision-making characteristic of particular styles, or levels, of leadership.

Three 'bandwidths' of decision-making

We shall define a *level of leadership* as the *bandwidth of decision-making, which predominates in the conduct of a leader.* The first level, inhabited by leaders whose decision-making lies predominantly between automatic and closed, we shall call *closed*. The second, in which decision-making characteristically falls between closed and open, we shall call *open*.

For the third level of leadership, in which decision-making is found predominantly on the axis between open and strategic, we shall apply the term *strategic* (see Figure 2.1).

Since these generic closed, open and strategic levels of leadership are visible in the activity of individual managers, of teams and of organizations, we shall assign additional terms to signify the three levels in each of these three specific contexts.

In the case of an individual manager, we shall use the terms passive, active and visionary. For a team, the three levels will be represented as static, dynamic and organic.

For a whole organization, we shall call the corresponding three levels of leadership culture past-oriented, goal-oriented and service- oriented (see Figure 2.2).

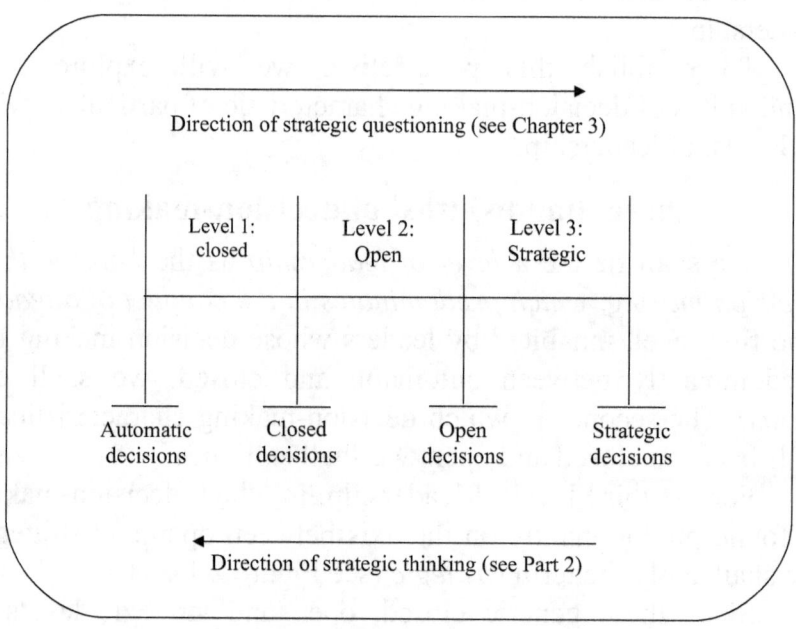

Figure 2.1 Three levels of leadership

Dimension	Manager/ leader	Team	Organization
3rd (Strategic)	Visionary	Organic	Service-oriented
2nd (Open)	Active	Dynamic	Goal-oriented
1st (Closed)	Passive	Static	Past-oriented

Figure 2.2 Three levels in three contexts

The development of the internal action - the culture - of an organization means development, first, in individual and then in team contexts. For both individual managers and teams, there is the possibility of moving between levels. Put very simply, as the managers in a team move from passive to active, the team as a whole may move from static to dynamic. When all the teams in an organization are dynamic, the organization itself can be goal-oriented, and so on.

To create an initial awareness of the differences that exist both in the quality of thought and in the quality of personal influence between the three levels of leadership, we shall concentrate on the context of individual managers - passive, active and visionary - and address three questions in respect of the vision within each level. First, how do they see their overall responsibility as leaders? Second, how do they judge the quality of a decision? Third, what do they consider to be important when running meetings?

Leadership Level 1: Closed/Passive Leadership

Generally speaking, the passive leader is unable to feel or to articulate a clear difference between responsibility and authority.

There is a fairly fixed set of established activities, and as long as these are carried out in the habitual way, responsibility is considered to be fulfilled - if it is considered at all. The passive leader sees the world as fixed. Change is an exceptional and undesirable phenomenon, and offers the greatest challenge to the level 1 leader: the status quo must vigorously be preserved and defended.

It is important to recognize that active and visionary leaders can also make decisions to resist change, but this will be for different reasons. The passive leader has no choice but to resist change, thanks to an inability to respond differently. This resistance will be evident in many aspects of external action, and perhaps most easily observable in conversation. Passive leaders often have two very noticeable habits in conversation. The first is a general defensiveness and tendency to apologize unnecessarily.

This may take the form of 'explaining' some aspect of inadequacy, of consistently answering unasked questions or of speaking compulsively about their opinions, possessions, memories, achievements, friends, families, concerns, fears and so on.

These aspects of faltering self-image can be reinforced by gossip about others.

The second habitual subject, closely related to the first, is talk about the past. Whole meetings go by in which the only subject is the past, and the only intention is an unarticulated wish to carry on living in it. The medium of language may itself contain a high proportion of clichés. If this description is becoming something of a caricature, it is only necessary to come into contact with a dozen or so boards of directors chosen at random from more or less anywhere in the world to recognize that a high proportion of senior positions are occupied by people who either have always been, or who have become, passive leaders.

How do passive leaders judge the quality of their decisions? Living in the past (which may take the form of living in a long-since-formed view of the future), they have a simple and reliable formula for what constitutes the criterion for a good decision: precedent. That is, the precedents they approve of!

Passive leaders, that is, leaders whose decision-making lies predominantly in the bandwidth between automatic and closed decisions, can be found in all walks of life and at all levels of organizations. Owing to their readiness to remain with one company, often coupled with strong ambition, they quite easily end up in senior positions. When this is the case, how do they run meetings?

Meetings run by passive leaders have two distinct peculiarities. The first is that the passive leader who is running the meeting does most of the talking. The second is that he or she is unaware of this, and will often have the impression that others have talked much more! Other characteristics follow. The most important aspect of meetings is considered to be discussion, irrespective of whether conclusions are reached. If conclusions are reached, they are unlikely to be converted into decisions, that is, to be the source of new action. Typically, the participants leave the meeting at least slightly disgruntled, with the exception of those already resigned to such a culture. Most significantly, nobody is asked to prepare for such meetings.

Taking the decision-making diagrams that we developed in Chapter 1, we can create a combined picture of the quality of personal, group and corporate decision-making typical of this closed level of leadership (see Figure 2.3).

Agenda for meetings, if they exist, are routine, and the major stimulus to thought is the perceived threat of change. The thinking itself takes the form of an unconscious clinging to precedent. Decision-making is in the range between automatic and closed. The quality of influence is static, or gradually deteriorating, and its impact is on external action only, which it seeks to confine to concordance with precedent. In line with precedent, many meetings in a closed leadership culture take place at a moment's notice, without agenda, in order to deal with an 'urgent problem' that has arisen due to unforeseen circumstances.

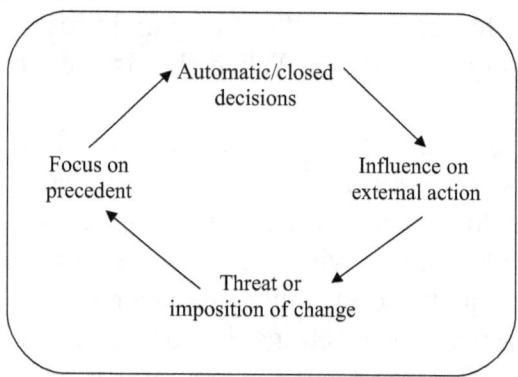

Figure 2.3 Closed leadership culture.

A further typical feature is that, where agenda exist, they are likely to focus on external action - what people have been doing and what they are going to do. This may be reflected in the minutes' of the meeting, which can even record, in narrative style, what everyone said.

While the range of thought, discussion, decisions and possible development for the passive leader is severely limited compared to that of the active leader, this does not mean that the passive leader is not busy. Far from it! The passive leader is much too busy to pay anything other than lip-service to the qualities and practices of the active leader, and to the possibility of development in such a direction.

Leadership Level 2: Active/Open Leadership

The active leader has a quite different feeling of underlying responsibility to that which features in the thought and meetings of a closed leadership culture. This centers around an attitude towards change. Where the passive leader denies change, the active leader recognizes that change is inherent in all aspects of life and appreciates that it is the inevitability of change that gives rise to the role of leader in the first place! Why should an owner, with a good business idea, go to the trouble and expense of employing managers to lead, if not because, over time, there will surely be changes both from within and from outside the business?

Aware of this, the active leader feels a need to develop a more effective relationship with the world of change. The sense of responsibility is transformed from resisting change to accepting, promoting and even creating change. Since the overused phrase managing change is so often applied in a sense which indicates the type of delayed reaction, crisis management or 'coping' characteristic of closed leadership, we shall adopt the term *governing change* to indicate the strong impulse that exists in the active leader, felt as a responsibility, to dominate and even control changes that take place in the area of his or her authority.

Almost in the same breath as recognizing this underlying responsibility, the active leader starts to become aware of personal and group shortcomings in terms of capacity to fulfill it. Suddenly, a new fact becomes clear: in order for this responsibility to be fulfilled, there must be an increase in the quality of personal and group influence. How can this be generated? Once this question starts to receive an open response, the open leadership culture can be pictured as a learning culture (see Figure 2.4). Because the active leader wishes to learn, new questions enter - open questions, which promote new directions of thought and discussion. When these combine with the feeling of responsibility to govern change, open decisions result - that is, decisions have not been made before and lead to new possibilities in the quality of influence.

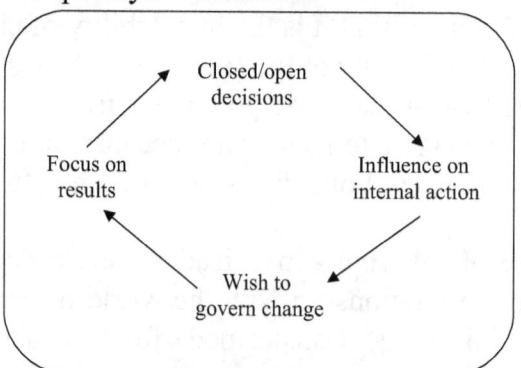

Figure 2.4 Open (learning) leadership culture.

When judging the quality of decisions, the active leader, like the passive leader, tends to look backwards. However, there is a difference. Whereas the passive leader looks to the time period before the decision was made, to search out precedent, the active leader is interested only in the time period between the making of the decision and its expected result. For whereas the passive leader influences activity, the active leader influences results, and will evaluate decisions on the extent to which they brought a certain result nearer.

When participating in meetings, there is again a significant difference. The active leader has started to learn in a way that has an impact on personal influence, and therefore on the quality of meetings. Increasingly aware of the nature and value of high-quality preparation, active leaders become ready to prepare as requested for meetings in which they participate, and to request preparation from participants when they are running meetings.

Depending on the quality of such preparation, the effectiveness of meetings and the subsequent quality of group influence can be dramatically improved.

The active leader values meetings by the same currency as decisions: their results. Minutes, if they exist, are therefore in the form of brief action lists, disseminated at the end of a meeting or very shortly afterwards as a reminder for those who have made commitments. If the culture is sufficiently open, there will be no need for minutes; new actions will simply enter the diaries of those responsible. And if anyone who attended did not leave the meeting with a specific action to perform, the active leader will review the necessity of their attendance next time or restrict the agenda to issues that concern the whole group.

As vision grows, the active leader discovers that, whereas

all previous meetings were broadly similar in character, it now becomes possible to differentiate between various types of meeting, depending on who the participants are and on what the relationship is in terms of authority. We shall explore these issues in detail in Chapter 6.

Leadership Level 3: Creative/Visionary Leadership

Between the culture of the second and third levels of leadership lies as big a gap as that between the first and second. At the core of this difference is a further quantum leap in how responsibility is felt and acted upon. To gain a picture of this, it will be useful to turn our attention to the framework of understanding that forms the backcloth to strategic leadership - a set of ideas that relate responsibility much more precisely to authority.

The visionary leader has an understanding, which can grow as a result of the continuation and fulfillment of the impulse experienced by the active leader as to govern change. In response to fundamental questions about the nature of the relationship between responsibility and authority, the active leader starts to realize that if harmony is to exist both within and between organizations, and within and between individuals, the feeling of responsibility must be related to the exercise of authority in a specific way. We shall call this the Principle of Strategic Responsibility.

The Principle of Strategic responsibility

This principle is based on the existence of the four underlying directions of personal influence in relation to authority, which we have already uncovered in Chapter 1. To examine this in more detail, let us take the example of a typical leader in a business organization, which has the traditional pyramid-like structure of authority.

Placed on, say, the third or fourth 'rung' of the hierarchy, the manager's influence is exerted in four directions: first, 'upwards', towards a superior, i.e. one who has greater authority; second, 'downwards', towards those under the manager's authority; third, 'sideways within the organization', towards colleagues; and fourth, 'sideways outside the organization', towards customers, suppliers, the marketplace, the labor market and the wider community.

By examining these relationships more closely in turn, it becomes possible to see clearly what is necessary on the part of the manager, from a generic point of view, in order that the relationship can be sustained and flourish. This will point to a definition of responsibility specific to the direction of influence.

Influencing 'downwards'

The nature of the leader's strategic responsibility towards reports starts to emerge when we picture the most common symptoms of the breakdown and failure of such relationships.

From the point of view of the report, the job 'isn't interesting or stimulating enough', there 'isn't clear enough direction or consistency from above', there is 'insufficient' - or too much - 'autonomy', the 'rewards are inadequate', the 'career path is uncertain', and so on.

From the point of view of the manager, the report 'performs inadequately', is 'not the right person for the job' or 'fails to fulfill potential'. Alternatively, when the relationship is terminated, 'budgets have to be cut', and so on.

All these frequently cited reasons for failure point to shortcomings on the part of the manager in relation to satisfying the requirements of a generic responsibility 'downwards', which we will define as: *to create and maintain the conditions in which potential will be fulfilled*. These conditions refer not only to the physical conditions of space and remuneration, but also to much more subtle aspects connected with the work environment and the harmonizing of the personal interest of the report with the corporate interests represented by the manager.

Influence 'upwards'

How, then, can we define the strategic responsibility 'upwards'? This responsibility will reflect a reciprocal relationship to the responsibility 'downwards', and we shall define it as: *to make a full contribution*. Again it is clear that, when there is a long-term failure in respect of meeting this responsibility, the grounds will exist for ending the relationship.

There are two further relationships in which the difference between levels of authority is nil. One is with colleagues in a peer group within the organization; the other is with people outside the organization.

Influence 'sideways' - Peer level influence

Taking first the relationship with colleagues, we can again ask the question: what is it that leads to the breakdown, or diminishes the effectiveness, of such relationships? Symptoms of such breakdown or ineffectiveness range from the absence of genuine contact and poor quality communication to èmpire-building' and active divisiveness - all contrary to the interests of the organization. Behind such symptoms lies one thing - an absence of mutual trust. The responsibility in this relationship is to counter the possible development of such a factor, and we shall define this 'sideways' responsibility as to generate mutual trust and cooperation.

External influence

There remains the fourth direction of influence, which is towards individuals from outside the organization and with whom no permanent differential is laid down in terms of level of authority. Let us take as an example the relationship with a customer. In the early stages of the relationship, the influence required may be similar to that towards a superior within the organization, i.e. to convince the (potential) customer of an ability to contribute (or, as the jargon has it, to 'add value').

As the relationship develops, it may start to resemble more closely the relationship between colleagues. While the customer retains the ultimate discretion as to the continuous renewal of the relationship, often what is sought by the customer as the relationship matures is colleague-like trust and cooperation rather than 'added value', which by now is taken for granted. Or we could say that the colleague-like trust and cooperation become the added value. And in the most secure customer relationships, the supplier helps fulfill the responsibility we have already ascribed to the leader - the creation and maintenance of the conditions for the fulfillment of potential. The more the supplier achieves this, the less likely will the customer decide to change the supplier.

When relationships with customers, suppliers, the labor market, the industry or the wider community break down, what is the universal result? In general, we can say that damage is done to the reputation of the organization. This gives us the strategic responsibility related to influence exerted on behalf of the organization: *to enhance the reputation of the organization.* Now we can assemble the complete picture of strategic responsibility (see Figure 2.5).

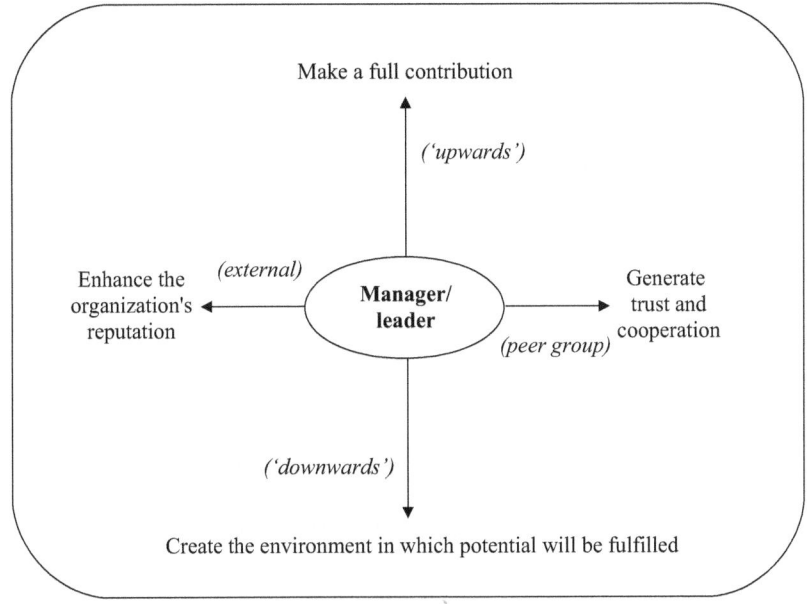

Figure 2.5 The Principle of Strategic Responsibility.

For the visionary leader, these four strategic responsibilities - to make a contribution (upwards), to generate trust and cooperation (peer group), to create the conditions in which others can fulfill potential (reports) and to enhance the organization's reputation (external) - constitute the fundamental guidelines for all decision-making. The underlying responsibility of strategic leadership is to *serve the four strategic responsibilities*.

In Figures 2.3 and 2.4, we created a picture of closed and open leadership culture. Now we can do likewise for strategic leadership culture (see Figure 2.6).

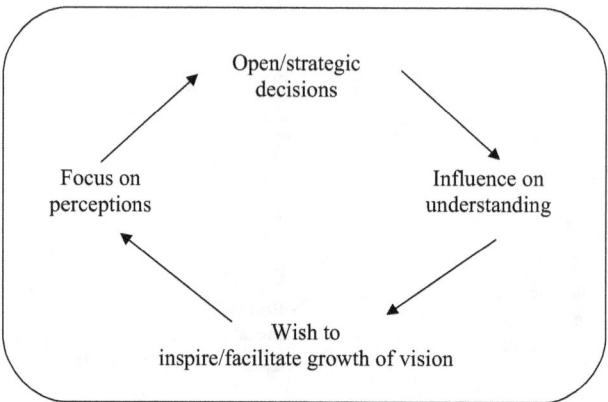

Figure 2.6 Strategic leadership culture

Strategic decision-making

We are now ready for a central definition. Strategic decision-making is the *alignment of open decisions with strategic responsibility.* It involves a process of articulating vision, defining purpose, creating aims and objectives and securing tactics. All decisions are made as part of, and with reference to, this strategy; and a strategy exists in respect of every decision the visionary leader makes.

At first, this may sound complicated, tortuous, difficult and unnecessary. To start with, as with developing any ability, it may indeed be like that. With practice, strategic decision-making can become second nature, creating an otherwise unsustainable level of flexibility and confidence. When strategic decision-making spreads through an organization, it generates a most subtle and powerful form of competitive advantage.

The visionary leader has a great advantage over both the passive and the active leader. For these latter can judge the quality of a decision only in hindsight. The visionary leader, in contrast, has paved the way in terms of strategic thinking in advance, so that decisions are much easier to find which meet the requirements of responsibility. In level 3 leadership decisions can be judged at the time they are made, on the basis of their likely capacity to contribute to one or more of the strategic responsibilities. In closed and open leadership, this is not possible because the strategic responsibilities have not been articulated in relation to the situation. Later, if the potential proves to be different from what was anticipated, the visionary leader's attitude allows this unexpected development to be treated simply as new information, which in turn may feed the next strategic question and decision.

This advantage has to be earned. The level 3 leader has often had to work hard to overcome painful barriers in improving both the quality of thought and the quality of personal influence. This results in a greater degree of objectivity so that, unlike the passive leader who influences external action, or the active leader who influences internal action, the creative/visionary level 3 leader is able to influence *understanding*.

In running meetings, the visionary leader is a facilitator and catalyst, operating with a priceless piece of practical knowledge - *how to get out of the way*. Results and other pieces of information are transmitted quickly or in advance: participants are invited to prepare new ideas for approval. The awareness of the active leader of different types of meetings has been developed first to a clear understanding of ten archetypes of business meeting, and then to a deeper level of understanding at which all meetings can be considered to be essentially of the same type.

The value of images

Understanding is a product of the relationship between vision and action. This means it cannot be directly transmitted from one person to another. Can you give another person your understanding of your favorite hobby, for example? Or of how to drive a car? Unlikely. You can tell them about it, and perhaps enthuse them to start taking an interest themselves. You might also show them something of the associated external action. This will be the beginning of creating the conditions in which they can develop their own understanding.

Since understanding is needed in order that potential can be fulfilled, it is part of the responsibility of a leader to create the conditions in which others can develop their own understanding. The creation of such conditions will include the exposure to new questions, leading to the assimilation of new information and ideas resulting in new decisions for practical experimentation. Without these ingredients, learning does not happen.

Images can be useful in the assimilation of ideas, and for this reason both diagrams and stories have been used in the first chapters of this book. Now we shall explore the possible value of another kind of image: an imaginary situation which has enough parallels with live management/leadership challenges to help develop a fuller picture of the detailed implications of ideas we have already discussed in outline.

Our image will be one of apparently very modest proportions - a situation in which any professional manager could be expected to excel! Yet despite its apparent simplicity, this exercise has been found revelatory by chief executives and senior management teams on both sides of the Atlantic.

The first five decisions

You are invited to put yourself in the position of the recipient of an imaginary letter reproduced in Example 2.1 from a friend, XL, who runs a Youth Club. XL is ill, and has written to you because you have agreed to take over the running of the Youth Club Holiday, which starts in eight days' time, on 10 July.

We shall also assume that you are unable to have any further communication with XL, other than to obtain the telephone numbers of everyone mentioned in the letter. For any other matters you rely on the information provided by XL in his letter and on the attached list of preparation items already completed or still to be done (Example 2.2).

This situation reflects business life in the sense that opportunities to create a strategy from scratch rarely exist. There is usually a past, which brings with it a legacy of resources and expectations.

How will you respond? It is recommended that, to get the most from this imaginary situation, you take the trouble to study the scenario and to work out the first five decisions you would take in this situation, together with the reasons for them.

A group of chief executives who worked on this exercise drew three key conclusions. First, they found that, working separately, they each came up with a list of 'first five decisions' which differed markedly from their colleagues' lists. Second, they could see that in some cases the list of decisions they had made reflected quite accurately their style of decision-making in business, and that in other cases the list represented an ideal, which they did not reach in business life. Third, they found after further discussion that there were aspects they had failed to consider which placed the whole situation in a new light.

Example 2.1

The Whinney
Old Nut Lane
Backwater
Nr Effingham
Surrey

Dear New Leader,

It's such a relief to know that you are taking over the running of the Youth Club Holiday, and I am sure that it will be a great success, knowing your interest in the work of the Federation as a whole, and the spirit of its motto: 'Social evolution through responsible living.'

As I mentioned, there were some difficulties on the last holiday, mainly because the six 17/18-year-olds are becoming uncontrollable. They are such a crazy bunch! Albert looks down on everybody else (and it will be worse now that he's passed his driving test and has his own car); Janet never stops checking her make-up, always goes on about shopping and seems to have a crush on Victor; Vic himself says he hates camping, especially the food (says he could do better himself!); Mandy is a total contrast, and holds everyone together with her tact and willingness to please; Jackie seems scatty---she's always imagining everything's going to be a disaster (a real hypochondriac!); and Bill, when he's not sloping off to the pub (a bad influence on the younger ones) is always playing practical jokes on everyone. (I'd actually like to expel Bill from the Club, but his father is a federation Vice-President.) The younger kids are generally good fun, except that they tend to divide into gangs and cliques under the influence of the older ones. My favorites are Sharon (14) and Mickey (15): they are always ready to help me do the important things like cooking and don't seem to mind the jeers of some of the others. There are about ten 15/16-year-olds and 14 younger ones.

You'll like the adult helpers: Helen (a great organizer---she really knows how to put the fear of god into the little brats!) and Peter (very experienced hill-walker: a great outdoors man!---even if the kids think he's crazy!). To strengthen the ranks, I've also arranged for Miranda (another adult), Toby and Annabelle (18-year-olds) to be there; they're from the TQ Camping Advisory Society, and know how to make sure that holidays are successful and conform to the required standards.

  Please find below a list of preparations already made and things still to be done.

  Good luck!

  XL

Example 2.1 (contd)

YOUTH CLUB HOLIDAY: PREPARATION

Already done	To be done prior to start of camp on 10 July	To be done at camp site (1st day)
• Contributions ($20 each) already collected from all parents. • Bank account opened to fund holiday • Camp-site deposit ($75) paid booked: 50% • $75 set aside for food • $75 set aside for transport, medical and contingency • $150 budgeted for hiring tents and equipment (would cost double to purchase---no funds for this) • $150 set aside to be paid to TQCAS	• Phone parents, find out who can give lifts • Design and send map to drivers • Do shopping (Sat?) • Hire tents, mobile cookers, gas canisters, etc. • Update medical equipment • Pay TQCAS deposit • Mend box	• Get Hazel to divide kids into small groups for activities until supper (TQCAS people to help?) • Do cooking (with Sharon). Organize • David to pitch tents (Madeleine and Micky to help?) • Organize wood for camp fire

  Following this, they developed together three archetypal ways of responding to the situation, which correspond to the three levels of leadership we have just explored. These three levels of response are reproduced here in order to clarify and elaborate on the essential differences between the four levels of decision-making.

  The response typical of the first level of leadership is illustrated below by the imaginary character L1, that of the second level by L2 and that of the third level by L3.

Route thinking: static influence

L1 has accepted XL's request to take over the running of the holiday because XL did him a similar favour a year or two ago.

Having taken it on, the first question that comes into L1's mind is: 'Do I know how to do this?' He quickly answers himself: 'No, I've never done anything like this before!'

He immediately summons another closed question: 'Do I know of anyone who does know how to run a Youth Club Holiday?' 'Yes', he answers himself, 'of course: Helen and Peter, the adult helpers XL mentioned in the letter!' Now on automatic pilot, he telephones Helen and Peter to see if they agree with him that it would be a good idea to have a meeting to plan the holiday.

They agree, and decide on which evening to meet. Helen also suggests that Miranda, Toby and Annabelle, from TQCAS, are invited, so L1 calls them: Toby and Annabelle can make it, but Miranda is away for a few days and cannot be contacted before the meeting.

L1's first concern at the meeting is to make sure that the preparation items listed in XL's letter are carried out. Most of the evening is spent locating the information that will enable L1 to do this: the telephone numbers of the parents; the main items of shopping; where to hire the equipment; the medical equipment that needs to be updated; and locating the box that needs mending.

Eventually, noticing that L1's workload is mounting, Annabelle volunteers to do the shopping, and Peter says he will organize the equipment. After some discussion - L1 wants to be sure they really don't mind - this is agreed. They also decide to contact each other by telephone to arrange a further meeting once Miranda is back.

A focus on perpetuation of the past

At this point, we can review the first five decisions made by L1 following his precedent-inspired acceptance of XL's request. First, a closed decision, driven principally by his own insecurity, to hold a meeting to discuss activity. Second, an automatic decision to follow XL's plan to the letter.

Third, a closed decision to accept proposals from Annabelle and Peter - driven by their perception of his weakness - to help with some of the tasks. Fourth, an automatic decision that L1 will carry out the remaining tasks himself. Finally, there is a decision which lies somewhere between automatic and closed, to delay any further arrangement until the return of Miranda - an event outside L1's influence.

Based on this conduct, we can easily interpret where L1 feels his responsibilities to lie. He has taken over in something of a crisis, and his duty is, to the best of his ability, to continue the planning and management of the holiday as if XL himself were in charge.

There is no doubting L1's good intentions! The limitations on the quality of his decision-making come precisely from this unarticulated sense of responsibility while, as we shall see, the authority he is given actually permits possibilities he could not dream of.

Crisis and survival

How will L1's decisions impact on others? Based on what we now know of him, let's project some aspects of the scenario still to unfold. He manages to carry out the tasks agreed at the meeting, as do Annabelle and Peter. Miranda returns and calls L1, upset to have been omitted from the meeting. He apologizes, explaining that XL had not told him she would be away. Eventually, she agrees to come to a second meeting, the next evening.

By now there are only three days before the holiday is due to start. The meeting is spent preparing a circular to be hand-delivered in the morning to all the kids explaining what they must bring and confirming travel arrangements. They agree to meet again the following evening to arrange all the activities for the first day of the holiday, since all feel that the kids must be kept fully occupied.

And so it continues. Everything that really has to be done for the survival of the holiday just about happens on time. L1 and his management team, as he likes to call his five helpers, spend long hours each night of the holiday planning the next day's activities and reviewing the youths' conduct.

Inevitably, there are discipline problems, and two of the older youths have to be sent home. Later, another two leave voluntarily. After it's all over, L1 meets XL for a beer and recounts a series of humorous incidents, not all of which were so funny at the time. . . .

Influencing internal action

L2 has responded to XL's request because she likes a challenge.

Knowing the value of preparation in all aspects of leadership, she sets aside an hour on the evening of 2 July to study XL's letter and enclosure and to formulate an initial plan. The question at the back of her mind as she reads is: `What will be my key objective in running this holiday?'

After some consideration, it is clear to her. Holidays should be enjoyable experiences, and it is clear from XL's letter that to create enjoyment for everyone will be a real challenge. Her objective then will be that everyone on the holiday will enjoy themselves.

Having written this down, L2 realizes that, while she's calling this an objective, it isn't one yet. At best, it could be called a quality objective, or an aim. But objectives, to be useful, must be concrete - that is, capable of measurement and therefore of monitoring and control. How can she measure people's enjoyment during the holiday?

Pondering this, L2 remembers an 'evaluation form' used during a leadership training course she once attended. This form invited participants, at the end of a session, to list the points they had found most interesting and useful, to make suggestions and other comments, and to grade the session 'excellent', 'very good', 'good', 'acceptable' or 'unacceptable'. Based on this, L2 decides to create her own 'enjoyment monitor'.

Orientation towards objectives

On a sheet of paper, L2 designs the five questions that will constitute the 'enjoyment monitor'. While based on her past experience, they are adapted to the new situation. First question: 'What were the four most enjoyable moments for you today?'

Second question: 'What gave you most enjoyment of all?' Third question: 'What did you least enjoy today, and how do you think this can be remedied?' Fourth question: 'Please indicate your level of enjoyment of the day as a whole' - followed by five categories to be ringed or ticked: 'Great fun', 'Good fun', 'OK', 'Boring', 'Miserable'. Fifth question: 'What other comments would you like to make about today?' The enjoyment monitor is now complete.

L2 can foresee that this management tool will be useful in a number of ways. First, the nature of the questions will promote a positive attitude among the youths, since attention will be focused on what they enjoyed. If there is dissatisfaction, this can be expressed in the form of suggested improvements.

There will also be a constant flow of information that will provide signals for management about who needs extra attention. To create a concrete measure of enjoyment, L2 decides to assign a numerical value for each of the categories to be ticked in question 4: 5 for Great fun, 4 for Good fun, 3 for OK, 2 for Boring and 1 for Miserable.

'Yes', L2 says to herself, 'this system will also help me to give feedback to parents about their kids, and it would be great if we could achieve an average of, say, 3.8 per child as a daily score for the whole holiday!' Just then, she feels a tinge of anxiety - is this really the best way to manage? However, it soon passes, and L2 continues her planning.

Questioning the past

L2 has already verified the financial information under the àlready done' column (Example 2.2). A question in her mind is whether or not to go ahead with the payment to TQCAS (Total Quality Camping Advisory Services).

She knows that quality is important, and feels that Miranda, Toby and Annabelle have valuable expertise - it just seems a shame to pay out £150 for their services which, if it could be saved, could be used to buy tents and equipment.

However, as it won't affect the kids' enjoyment this time whether the equipment is owned or rented, and since the TQCAS members could add to the fun, she decides to pay the deposit.

Motivation through involvement

Having decided on the key objective - an average daily enjoyment rate of 3.8 per child - L2 starts to plan the route towards this. Given the time constraints, she is inclined to take XL's character assessment at face value, and feels that the best management team will probably be herself plus the three adults - Peter, Helen and Miranda - with Toby and Annabelle as assistants.

However, she would like to meet them in order to be sure before deciding on responsibilities. After that, it will be possible to set in motion the allocation of tasks, duties and activities for the holiday that will allow the youths to participate constructively. For L2 knows how closely involvement is related to motivation.

When telephoning the three adults and two assistants to invite them to a meeting, L2 also asks each of them to put some thought into ways of creating enjoyment for kids on such a holiday, and to bring four or five concrete ideas to the meeting.

Discussion of these prepared items quickly builds a constructive mood during the meeting - despite Miranda's absence - so that when L2 asks Helen and Peter to take specific responsibility for cooking and outdoor activities respectively and to base their planning on their own prepared suggestions, they readily agree.

L2 also explains her enjoyment monitoring system which, after initial resistance, is accepted as a good idea - so much so, that the members of the management team decide they will fill in the forms too!

Planning the planning

A further meeting is set for detailed planning in two days' time, at which Helen and Peter agree to present considered ideas on activity schedules and on how the kids will be divided into teams, based on what is known of their talents, inclinations and friendships.

It is also agreed that Toby and Annabelle will take care of the remaining items of preparation on XL's list and make all transport arrangements.

In order to undermine any possible resistance from Miranda on her return, L2 writes to her immediately after the meeting giving details of the decisions reached and asking her to telephone on her return. When she telephones, L2 plans to ask Miranda what responsibilities she would like to have.

Decisions of a Level 2 Leader

Let us pause to review L2's first five decisions. First, an open decision resulting in an overall objective for the holiday which can be measured and monitored. Second, a closed decision to retain the TQCAS arrangements already in place - plus XL's character assessments.

Third, an open decision for a well-prepared meeting as the first step towards achieving the overall objective. Fourth, the generation of decisions in the closed/open bandwidth for actions by each participant at the meeting.

Fifth, an open decision to reduce possible negativity from Miranda on her return by acknowledging her potential value and by focusing attention on future possibilities through inviting her to define her own participation.

A different vision - with possibilities for new action and results

The amount of detail in these imaginary scenarios is perhaps just enough for us to be able to taste the gulf that separates the quality of decision-making of L2 from that of L1.

While L1's sense of responsibility is all about preservation and projection of the past, L2 feels a responsibility to secure the future in a way that requires active, planned influence on her part.

Her awareness of aspects of the energies that drive people, and her sensitivity to the balance that a leader needs to strike between clear direction on the one hand and autonomy on the other, mean that she addresses questions to which L1 is oblivious. Consequently her decisions, and the quality of her personal influence, are of a different order.

Projecting further developments for L2 as we did for L1, we can envisage that, by the time the holiday starts, a certain level of organization will have been achieved. Activities will have been planned in some detail for each day of the holiday, with room for ad hoc adjustments, additions and deletions: the management team will most likely have the time to be able to follow up their inclination and intent to create enjoyment, and it could well happen that L2's objective of 3.8 may be exceeded!

Motivation or manipulation?

Before turning to a possible Level 3 Leadership response, let us consider the moment of uncertainty when L2 asked herself whether the 'enjoyment monitor' really was such a good idea. What was going through her mind?

Many organizations use systems of personality profiling, performance appraisal, salary review and even recruitment which aim to make human potential manageable according to some universal formula. L2's 'enjoyment monitor' is representative of such attempts.

There can be something in such systems that is restrictive, manipulative and consequently demotivating in character. Their use can also indicate the absence of certain human qualities which, if present in the leadership culture, would render such complex and inevitably limited systems quite unnecessary.

Perhaps we can learn something about this from L3.

Level 3 Thinking, Decision-making and Influence

L3's motives for agreeing to run the holiday are quite different. After all, L3 takes his investment of time very seriously. He even acknowledges time as the most finite of all the finite resources available to him. While his response to XL's request has been immediate and unqualified, it reflects years of rigorous self-questioning about how to live in a productive way and to exert a constructive influence.

The last part of XL's first paragraph re-awakens the motive which inspired him to agree to the request, and, as he reads the letter, his eyes linger on the words: 'motto: Social evolution through responsible living.'

Behind these words he can feel so clearly the inspiration of the founders of the Federation of Youth Clubs, a vision of the relationship between attitude and conduct, and of the responsibility every generation has for the quality of the next. Yes, this is a vision with which he is more than ready to align his personal efforts.

In due course, L3 will study the rest of XL's letter. When he does, it will be primarily to learn about XL, and to evaluate the content of the letter against the implications of the motto which underpins the Youth Club's formation and very existence.

While he will then absorb the information contained in the letter more fully than either L1 or L2, he will always measure this against the flavor of XL's attitude of conflict, difficulty and fear - factors which have now resulted in incapacity for XL and potential chaos for those over whom he has authority. Chaos on which they will not be able to thrive!

The beginnings of strategic thinking

On receiving the letter, L3 settles into a relaxed mode of contemplation. Over the years he has learned the great value, when accepting any project, of first taking time to define the purpose of his involvement - only in this way can he be sure that his actions will have meaning.

So he asks himself what can be the nature of his contribution - that is, how can he serve the responsibility 'upwards?' To provide relief for XL is one aspect, but he would not undertake this venture just for that. His definition of purpose has to be based on a higher vision represented in this case by the motto he has just been reading.

As he ponders, L3 gives himself a working definition of purpose, which he formulates as 'to assist in the development of responsible future citizens'. Towards fulfilling this purpose, he creates three strategic aims: first, to create conditions, during the holiday, in which kids belonging to the Youth Club can learn to be more responsible; second, to create all-year-round opportunities to reinforce and enhance such learning; third, to create a reputation for the Club which will constantly attract new members.

Reviewing these initial components of his strategy, L3 checks that he is encompassing the four directions of responsibility. The statement of purpose, once agreed with the parents, will constitute at least a definition of the contribution he is to make; the first aim addresses the strategic responsibility 'downwards'; the second will require him to generate much higher levels of trust and internal cooperation than are currently in place; and the third will correspond to the 'sideways external' responsibility to enhance the reputation of the organization.

What will be his first objective? Wishing to have the direction of his planning authorized, and at the same time to set in motion the development of a more active relationship 'upwards', L3 decides that he must have contact, discussion and agreement with a quorum of parents which he will set at a minimum of 8 (out of a total of some 40 kids) within the next 48 hours. This, he notes, is concrete - as an objective always must be: measurable and controllable over time.

What, then, will be his tactics towards achieving this objective? He could refer to the list of parents' telephone numbers and call them himself. But he feels uneasy about this: it is so time-consuming, and surely there must be a way of working towards this objective which also contributes to one or more of the other strategic aims?

Strategic decision-making

Scanning XL's letter, L3 is struck by the description of Mandy, who apparently 'holds everyone together with her tact and willingness to please'. Perhaps she is a person, L3 thinks, who could in due course take on a public relations role with the parents. Why not first test her potential with a small task?

He telephones her, introduces himself and explains that one of the aims of the holiday is that the more senior kids will have the opportunity for greater responsibility. Would she like to have a responsible role? Mandy would.

L3 then explains his objective in relation to the parents, and checks that Mandy understands this. L3 asks her opinion of the best way to proceed. After some thought, Mandy suggests that she telephones the parents (she knows where to obtain a list) with a view to arranging a meeting for as many as can attend the following evening, and arranging times for L3 to speak by telephone to those who cannot make the meeting but would like to discuss the arrangements.

L3 says this is a good plan, makes sure she needs no further help, and they agree that she will call him back in a few hours. Two hours later, Mandy calls to say that the parents of six of the kids would like to attend the meeting, and the parents of another eight kids would like to speak with L3 during the following day.

L3 congratulates Mandy on this result. He has already decided, before this telephone call, that if she achieves the minimum target of arranging contact for him with the parents of eight kids, he will take a further step towards giving her greater authority, by inviting her to the meeting with the parents and involving her in both the planning and the subsequent decision-making.

By now, L3 has made two decisions, both of them strategic, each with a high quality of preparatory thought: first, to establish direct contact with a representative body of parents; second, to involve Mandy in the process. Meantime, while Mandy has been calling the parents, L3 has been making further decisions. Before we investigate these, let us pause to analyse some important components of L3's thinking.

The components of strategic thinking

The strategic decision-maker starts from vision, which we have defined as *knowledge of relatedness.* In the scenario in question, L3 takes the Youth Club motto as his vision. On this he is able to base the thought processes that will lead to strategic decisions and influence.

Beginning with the strategic responsibility upwards, he ponders how to define his purpose. We have already defined *purpose* (also sometimes called *mission*) as the *contribution of a lower authority in respect of a higher authority.*

Having defined purpose in relation to his specific situation, L3 then creates *strategic aims* which are similar adaptations to his situation of the remaining three strategic responsibilities. We have already defined strategic aims as *signposts for action to fulfill the purpose.*

The strategic decision-maker now converts one or more of the strategic aims into *objectives*, that is, into *concrete measures of productivity in relation to aim.* L3 decided on an objective of making direct contact with eight kids' parents within 48 hours.

To achieve this objective, he develops *tactics*, that is, the *application of resources to secure the objective.* In the case of L3, the tactics included strategic decisions about the use of his own time and about his personal influence. Interestingly, as we shall see, his *tactics* in the pursuit of one strategic aim have overlapped with an *objective* towards another strategic aim.

Strategy and time

The components of strategy of which a brief outline has been given above - *vision, purpose (or mission), strategic aim, objective and tactics* - give the possibility of a clear order of decision-making in relation to time. This order can be seen from two points of view: the order of planning, and the order of permanence (see Figure 2.7).

In strategic decision-making, the elements in order of permanence are vision, strategic aim, objective and last, tactic. This, therefore, is also the order of initial decision-making in any situation, as the example of L3 has shown.

The reverse will give the order of checking or reviewing decisions, and the order of subsequent change. Reflected in this order is the degree of concreteness, or the degree of measurability. The shorter term elements - objectives and tactics - are relatively concrete; the longer term elements - vision, purpose and aim - are relatively non-concrete.

Figure 2.7 Relative order and permanence

When it is well structured, such order can give an individual, a group or an organization a valuable balance of permanence and flexibility in relation to all decision-making.

Overlapping components

We have followed a line of L3's thought which derived from his articulation of upwards responsibility, or purpose.

Having formulated this as 'to assist in the development of future responsible citizens', he aims to have his planning for this authorized and, at the same time, to start an active relationship with the parents. He then sets himself an objective - to speak with a certain number of parents within a specified time - and involves Mandy in the tactics to achieve this objective.

Exploring another line of thought, we shall realize that there is an overlap. Pondering on his formulation of the strategic responsibility downwards - that is, the strategic aim to create conditions, during the holiday, in which kids belonging to the Youth Club can learn to be more responsible - L3 quickly concludes that the first step must be to give clear lines of authority through which the feeling of responsibility can be developed. It seems clear from XL's letter that very little authority has previously been given - a fact closely linked, in L3's view, to the leadership difficulties XL has faced.

Even on a first reading of XL's letter, L3 is already considering the suitability of the six 17-18-year-olds as team leaders. They clearly have an influence over the younger kids - hence the cliques. L3 also knows that most projects can be broken down into around six main functions, and this one is no exception: he quickly lists transport, provisions, cooking, accommodation (including safety), entertainments and PR (with the parents).

Based on XL's information, which L3 will wish to check for himself through contact with the kids, it seems already that the six older kids may have talents and inclinations which, if his influence is effective, will enable L3 to allocate authority for each of these main functions.

With this aim in mind, he resolves to make immediate contact with each of the kids and test his or her capability. Thus his interaction with Mandy, which we have already outlined, involves a tactical decision towards his objective for the parents and simultaneously helps him achieve an objective in relation to the kids.

'Total quality' management

Like L2, L3 is quick to question XL's preparation items, including the matter of the payment for TQCAS (Total Quality Camping Advisory Services). Unlike L2, L3 can make an immediate decision on this issue, based on strategic aim. For him, the presence of so-called quality experts may easily work against the very improvements he wishes to bring about.

Indeed, he is highly suspicious of the very notion that quality is something 'separate'. While an organization such as TQCAS may compensate, at least for a time, for the kids' lack of feeling of responsibility, this will never be a permanent solution, and may even prove counter-productive. So he decides to discontinue the relationship with TQCAS and use the money saved to purchase equipment that would otherwise have to be rented.

Concerning the adult helpers, he will decide on their roles

once he is in a position to determine finally the extent of authority that can be given immediately to the senior kids. In principle, he will treat them as colleagues, and encourage them to provide whatever help the senior kids need in fulfilling their roles.

Strategic communication

Again, the details of this imaginary scenario are perhaps just complete enough for us to be able to recognize the huge difference in quality of thinking between L2 and L3.

|Leadership Level 3 is separated from Level 2 by a vast gap in understanding and vision, and consequently also in speed of thought - for L3 will have needed only a few minutes to think through and reach decisions that have taken us pages to describe.

In addition to the contrasts in thinking and decision-making in the responses of closed, open and strategic leadership in a given situation, there are equally significant differences in the quality of communication. We shall take as an instance the above example of delegation, in which L3 gave Mandy the authority - to which she was duly able to respond - to telephone parents on his behalf. How did he influence her, and what would be the likely approach of closed and open leadership in such a situation?

L3 began by explaining to Mandy his *strategic aim* concerning greater responsibility, and asked whether she was interested to work towards this. When she agreed, he then communicated his *objective* - to speak to the parents of eight kids within 48 hours. Then he asks for *her* input for the way forward.

Following her own suggestion, Mandy works towards *her*

own objectives: to arrange a meeting for the following evening, and to make up the minimum of eight sets of parents, plus any others, by arranging telephoning times - all within two hours! To achieve these objectives, she needed her own tactical steps: finding a list of telephone numbers, making the calls, and so on.

If we place the components of Mandy's thought and influence against those of L3, we shall see that there is a correlation which is fundamental in the development of strategic thinking and decision-making.

The issue that constitutes a strategic aim for L3 forms a statement of *purpose* for Mandy; and an objective for L3 is an *aim* for Mandy. These are the two areas in which the strategic thinking of these two individuals, who have different levels of authority, can overlap.

(L3 also has the option of communicating his own *purpose*, which would be, for Mandy, a statement of *vision*, but he chooses not to do so at this point, feeling that she is not yet ready to understand it and that, in any case, it will eventually require a more detailed face-to-face meeting.)

It is precisely this overlap which creates strength in the communication, and is the hallmark of an organization that is able to operate strategically. In order to fulfill her own aim - L3's objective - Mandy creates her own objectives and tactics.

We should note that, in real corporate life, such a level of sophistication is likely to be reached only after considerable development work has taken place, rather than on the immediate arrival of a strategic decision-maker indicated in this imaginary scenario.

By contrast, let us picture briefly how L1 and L2 might communicate in such a situation, and surmise what would consequently be the quality of their influence. Of course, the situation would never be quite the same, since it would have been reached differently. But let us assume that, as L3 has done, they each decide to delegate to Mandy the authority to communicate with parents. How will they implement this transfer of authority?

L1 is focused on external action. He cannot communicate purpose, strategic aim or objective because he has not formulated them for himself. The nearest he might come to it, in his own thinking, would be to decide that he *must* speak to as many parents as possible as soon as possible!

So he will give Mandy an order, or instructions: please telephone as many parents as possible as soon as you can. He will probably also tell her where to get the telephone numbers, and what to say. Despite his good intentions, his fear and personal insecurity, coupled with his blindness both to the abilities of others - actual and potential - and to the effect he has on them, will lead him onwards towards an inevitable crisis in the relationship with Mandy - a relationship he is hardly aware exists.

L2 comes somewhere between these two extremes, and a certain amount will depend on how far along the spectrum of open leadership she has progressed. A possible scenario, if she is quite far advanced, is that she communicates the same *objective* to Mandy as L3 - that is, direct contact for her with a minimum of eight sets of parents within 48 hours.

The remainder of the detail may follow as with L3, or she may involve herself more in the route to the objective, in the style of L1. An important question is: what happens if Mandy is unable to secure this objective?

In L2's book, this must be a failure. The objective was there, and it hasn't been met - which is less than motivating for all concerned. For L3, the fact that the objective is missed is not the end of the world, nor is it for Mandy if L3 is managing her, for he has already communicated his purpose and aim, which are still in force!

So what for L1 and L2 is a failure, for L3 and anyone who gradually adopts his way of thinking is no more than new information which is valuable for future decision-making towards strategic aim in fulfillment of purpose. Owing to the quality of his initial communication, he will find it much easier than L2 to re-motivate Mandy.

A new definition of leadership

A careful study of the differences between the three levels of leadership - even a study on such an imaginary scenario as this Youth Club Holiday - reveals the existence of very different underlying attitudes which are based not on experience, qualifications or conventional estimations of intelligence, but on much more subtle relationships between awareness, ability and action.

While it might be easy to categorize such awareness under 'people skills', such facile categorization can itself be indicative of a first level, or closed, mentality.

What is at stake here is our understanding of leadership. We can reach a new definition: *leadership is the ability to bring about and sustain a movement from a lower level to a higher level.* From the point of view of Leadership Level 3, the other two Levels are not really leadership at all.

Becoming and remaining a leader requires the continuous

growth of vision - for individual managers, for teams and for whole organizations. And for vision to grow, it must expand in two directions more or less simultaneously: towards a bigger picture of current and potential influence in life, and towards a much greater attention to the quality of detail in apparently small matters.

Fluctuation between levels

In painting a picture, during this chapter, of the three levels of leadership, we have necessarily discussed them in isolation, as if a manager or team occupies a particular level all the time. In reality, there is constant fluctuation between levels, and many gradations within them. At different moments in the course of a single meeting, it is quite possible for each participant to speak from the point of view of different levels.

It is important to appreciate that the level of a team or organization is always reduced to the level of its weakest member. For a team to be organic, all its members must be strategic. For an organization to be service-oriented, all groups within it must be organic.

It may be helpful - and is often necessary from the point of view of potential development - if a manager or group can find out which bandwidth of decision-making (i.e. level of leadership) they generally occupy. Once this is known, the meaning of possible development becomes clearer. And the very fact that it is known means that vision has already started to grow.

CHAPTER 3

The Growth of Leadership Vision

We have defined vision as knowledge of relatedness. We have also glimpsed the possibility that this knowledge can grow, and that the growth of vision has an impact on attitude and on internal and external action. Strategic decision-making demands and stimulates such growth.

We need to know how vision grows, and in what circumstances. First there is a more fundamental question: Does vision grow? Looking back over our lives or careers, we may see that vision has grown in that time. Certainly, at least, it has changed; but is change the same as growth? If a manager has 20 years of experience, has it really been twenty years, or one year 20 times?

Change ≠ Growth

A teenager sees a sports car and sets his heart on owning it. At the age of 22, he finally buys one, winning the envy of his friends and a succession of attractive companions. At 28, he feels a need for a more mature image, and buys a saloon car. At the age of 32, he swaps this for a car with the colors his bride prefers. At 40, with four young kids, he and his wife opt for a camper, rather than a saloon, for the sake of family holidays and outings.

From the point of view of external action, there has been a succession of changes. From the point of view of internal action, there may or may not have been any change. We cannot tell from the external actions alone.

One possibility, for example, is that between the second and third purchases, the young man saw that his choice of car had hitherto been heavily influenced by his desire for approval from others. Seeing the nature of that desire - an aspect of his own internal action and the attitude behind it - may have freed him from it to some extent in subsequent choices.

What's important is that the growth of vision requires a questioning of both external and internal action. This applies equally for individuals, groups and organizations. We shall call this process of the growth of vision: strategic questioning.

Strategic questioning: the process of growth

Strategic questioning is to do with the development of a greater receptiveness and sensitivity. For an individual, a group or an organization, this will mean an increased awareness of internal action and of attitude (Figure 3.1).

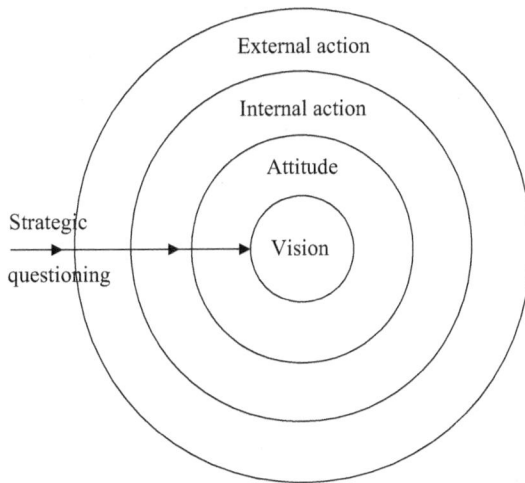

Figure 3.1 Strategic questioning: the process through which vision grows

79

In Figure 1.5 we saw that there is a qualitative relationship between decision-making by organizations, by groups and by individuals. Decision-making by organizations cannot be better than the decision-making by groups within it, and decision-making by groups cannot be better than the decision-making of the individuals within the group.

The same applies with asking questions. The strategic questioning ability of the organization as a whole cannot be better than that of the groups within it, which in turn cannot be better than that of the individuals within the groups.

This indicates in principle what is necessary for improvement. If the strategic questioning and decision-making capability of an organization is to be raised, the same capability must be raised at group level, and if this is to happen, the capability must be raised at individual level.

Barriers to the growth of vision

We have established in principle that vision can grow in certain circumstances, and that this growth requires an awareness and detached observation of both internal and external action.

To understand more about the nature of the growth of vision and the circumstances in which this can take place, we shall focus first on the ways in which it is prevented.

Unawareness of internal action

The first and most powerful barrier to the growth of vision is that we do not see our own internal action. If we could, and if we could remain aware of it on a daily basis, we might more easily stay interested in what kind of internal action we have, what influences it, and what other possibilities there might be.

Generally, we do not do this.

As a consequence, we believe in the products of our internal action - all our assumptions and prejudices - which are thus allowed to usurp the place of vision. As the pressures of life mount, these unseen prejudices and assumptions can become more and more rigid and, at the same time, even less visible and harder to question.

Not seeing our own internal action, we are equally unaware of the attitudes behind it, which tend to remain similarly unquestioned. These tendencies at individual level are often multiplied, amplified and even mutually reinforced in groups and whole organizations.

No time for growth

Because we do not see the existence of our internal action and attitudes, we fail to allocate time to observing them and bringing them into question. As a consequence, we do not engage in the process of strategic questioning outlined above. What may happen instead is that a contradiction gradually builds up between our assumptions and prejudices and our activity, or the activity of others. We may not see this happening. The contradiction grows and eventually there may be a crisis, a breakdown, an argument, stress, and conflict.

What happens within an individual also happens in groups. It can be alarming to see the speed of development of hostilities within an otherwise friendly group of people, simply through not allowing time for different interpretations to be exchanged.

Try explaining to a group of ten managers that an important financial decision depends on their ability to assess accurately, and as quickly as possible, how many squares there are in Figure 3.2.

Within seconds they are arguing. Two or three, pleased to remember that 4 x 4 = 16, say 'Sixteen!' Two or three others have quickly seen that the whole shape is a square, too. They shout 'Seventeen!' Others, who have stayed quiet, notice that each quarter of the whole shape is also a square. This makes four more squares. They shout 'Twenty-one!' The shouts of 'Sixteen!' gradually fall away, to be replaced by heated discussion about how there could possibly be 21 squares. Eventually, the pride which generates a tendency to cling to original estimates subsides in favour of a more objective interest in the total number of squares, which turns out to be 30.

Figure 3.2 How many squares?

This is how apparently intelligent, educated, senior executives can actually behave when confronted with a simple two-dimensional diagram! What does this say for the quality of decision-making in business life, where time is still more pressured and where the recipients of the impact of executive vision - people - are immeasurably harder to estimate and understand?

Being right

When internal action and attitude go unobserved, and when time is not dedicated to strategic questioning, then a third barrier to the growth of vision will inevitably arise: *the need to be right.* If we see it one way, and they see it another, then we must be right and they must be wrong. Our assumptions and prejudices defend the position they have taken, secretly knowing that the only alternative is horrendous crisis. A lifetime of self-justification may result.

Vision is thus prevented from growing, in individuals, groups and organizations alike, by a failure to acknowledge the reality of internal action, by a consequent failure to invest time and energy in exploring it, and by the resulting narrowing influence of an attitude of self-righteousness.

Vision, in other words, is prevented from growing by its own absence - by blindness! And even when there is an acknowledgement in principle of the possibility of the growth of vision, there are further blocks.

Blind to our own potential growth

There are two further barriers, which impede the dedication of time to the growth of vision. One is the fact that, by definition, we cannot see the path of our own development. We are blind both to what we need and to the nature of the process through which we can find it.

At the same time, we may instinctively distrust the ability

of business schools and conventional sources of management wisdom to provide what we need. This conviction may be reinforced by the silent memory that our formal education rarely, if ever, addressed this topic which now appears paramount: the growth of vision.

A special decision is needed

The fifth barrier to the growth of vision is that a special *decision* is needed for it. The four barriers already discussed make it most unlikely, for example, that a group of executives will agree to decide on a vision expansion initiative in which they will jointly participate.

The decision for it must be made or inspired by a leader. In most cases, this means a person senior in authority, and it is unlikely that such a person will make a decision for such investment of time by more junior executives unless they have themselves experienced and benefited from a similar initiative.

This factor applies all the way up the organization: therefore, a strategic attitude towards the growth of vision throughout an organization - which will always define the level of strategic decision-making within it - is only likely to take place in organizations in which the most senior decision-maker(s) are *already* in the habit of working actively on the growth of their personal vision.

This means that, for many organizations, a service-oriented leadership culture will never be achieved.

The conditions for growth

Bearing in mind these five barriers, we can explore in general terms the conditions, which make possible the growth of vision, and how they vary between the three Levels of Leadership.

Once internal action starts to become visible, then it is also possible to perceive two fundamental types of situation (see Figure 3.3). In the first type, there is a correspondence between vision and action. Knowledge of relatedness is in harmony with, or 'equal to' action. In this equation we may also include the *consequences* of action.

A simple example, in business terms, might be that a picture of the company's relatedness to its marketplace (vision) is represented by a financial budget (consequence of internal action), which is met (consequence of external action).

Alternatively, a new recruit achieves just the kind of performance which those involved in the recruitment process were seeking. Broadly we can say that equality between vision and action indicates a state of satisfaction.

In human experience, the second situation - an inequality between vision and action - seems to be more common! Simple examples might be missing a train, or having an accident. It is remarkable how we constantly provide for ourselves situations, such as new challenges, which give us the opportunity for vision and action to become unequal! When this is the case - when vision and action are in disharmony - *there are only three possible outcomes* (Figure 3.3).

Only 3 possible outcomes:

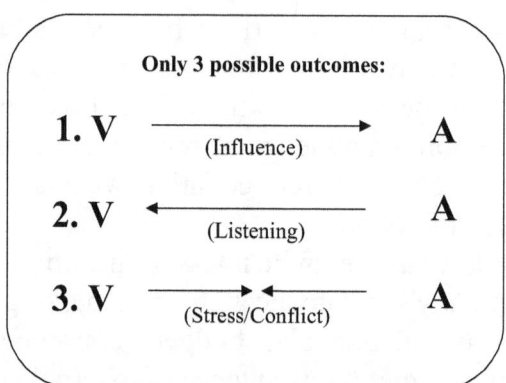

Figure 3.3 When vision ◊ action

In outcome 1, vision stays, and the (internal or external) action changes. For example, a couple orders a bottle of red wine while dining out. The waiter brings white wine by mistake. They insist: we asked for red! The waiter replaces the white wine with red.

In outcome 2, the action stays, and we adapt vision. The couple accepts the white wine, complimenting the waiter on his recommendation. (At the end of the meal, he offers them a complimentary digestive!)

In outcome 3, there is an incapacity to adapt vision, and the action cannot be altered. The couple insists on red wine, and there is only white! The inevitable consequence: argument, conflict, stalemate - *stress*.

There are no other possible outcomes! When there is disharmony between vision and action, only three results are possible: a different action, a crisis, or an adjustment of vision.

And since the ability to influence a change of action may depend in any case on the ability to adapt vision, this adaptation - the process of growth we have called strategic questioning - can be regarded as the key to a happy existence.

What part does it play in the three levels of leadership we have articulated: closed, open and strategic?

The growth of vision in a closed leadership culture

We have defined a closed/passive leadership culture as the level of leadership inhabited by managers whose decision-making lies predominantly in the bandwidth between automatic and closed.

Passive managers tend to relate responsibility to the fulfillment of an established set of habitual activities. The quality of decisions is judged primarily on their degree of concordance with precedent, and discussion is regarded as more important than its outcome. Change is generally treated (whether this is perceived or not) as threat, often the cause of much agitation, urgency and 'being busy'.

In this closed level of leadership, vision exists as a negative, a kind of minus quantity. In place of vision, the impostors prejudice and assumption are projected onto every situation, without their owners realizing this is happening. This can continue for months, years, even decades - until there is a crisis.

Negativity in vision is reflected also in negativity of attitude. The impossibilities in a situation take precedence over the possibilities.

Fear of negative outcomes removes any apparent risk from the agenda. The lack of absorption and digestion of experience through the process of strategic questioning is balanced by the growth of gossip, politics and internal empire-building.

In the advent of crisis, when the citadel of the past is under siege, vision may have an opportunity to grow. The opportunity may or may not be taken. The individual, group or organization may collapse under the pressure. The crisis may pass, to be followed by a return to the old way; or a kind of patching-up job is done.

In other cases, the crisis yields a degree of strategic questioning which may mark the first step of the transition towards an open leadership culture.

The growth of vision in an open leadership culture

We have defined an open/active leadership culture as the level of leadership inhabited by managers whose decision-making lies predominantly in the bandwidth between closed and open.

In this second level, leaders recognize that all their actions carry an influence, and feel a responsibility to influence effectively - to govern change. Aware that their ability to do so is limited, they look for ways to become more effective in their influence. Both decisions and meetings are judged by the results they generate.

When results are out of harmony with plans or intentions, the level 2 leader is presented with an opportunity for vision to grow. At the lower end of the open leadership spectrum, this opportunity may be ignored in favour of a show of power. At the upper end of the spectrum, imbalances between plan and result, between expectation and outcome, are seen and treated as learning opportunities which carry valuable information.

Because of the way such imbalances are seen, they generate

open questions which can lead to a forward-looking assessment of possibilities. Where the vision of the closed leader is rooted in the external action of the past, the vision of the open leader has a future orientation and includes an awareness of internal action.

The growth of vision in a strategic leadership culture

The third level of leadership is the only one in which the process of strategic questioning, as defined above, is an ingrained habit. The external action of the level 3 leader is connected to, and deliberately influences where possible, the growth of others' vision.

To serve the Principle of Strategic Responsibility, though it may not be articulated as such, is considered to be the prime responsibility, and decisions are evaluated by their capacity to contribute towards this. Meetings are regarded and used as vehicles for the growth of vision.

In strategic decision-making, the primary sources of information for decision-making may often be the attitudes and internal action evident in those occupying positions related to the visionary leader through the Principle of Strategic Responsibility.

Vision grows because the process of its growth is known and has become the central focus of both internal and external action. Thus the first barrier to the growth of vision - unawareness of internal action - has been overcome, perhaps permanently. Time is consequently dedicated to the growth of vision as a matter of course. The third barrier, the attitude of righteousness, has lost its power.

The vision of the closed leader looks to the past; that of the open leader looks to the future; but the vision of the visionary leader is rooted in the present. The past is seen in terms of its current legacy: the future is seen in terms of current potential. The topics of conversation change accordingly. Gossip and politics are seen as a waste of precious resources. Always present is the question: How can we contribute to the growth of vision, *now*?

Strategic thinking

For vision to start to grow, and for a strategic leadership culture to develop, a new quality of thinking is needed. As this new quality of thinking starts to pervade an organization, the entrenched ways of operating are uncovered, scrutinized, evaluated against new criteria and either discarded or continued and developed with a new vitality.

Once strategic decision-making forms the basis of the organization's action, this process of self-improvement and renewal can become an integral part of its operation. What is this new quality of thinking?

To create an initial distinction, we shall imagine two families embarking on an apparently similar, but in reality very different, day out. Each family consists of four people: the parents and two kids, aged 9 and 11. Each is setting out by car on a 3-hour journey to the same well-known leisure park for kids, where there are all kinds of fun activities. Everyone is looking forward to being there.

The parents of Family A promised the kids this trip some time ago, as an incentive for them to make the effort to write a story about their activities - part of their homework during the school holidays. Neither of them has written the story yet, but even so the parents feel they cannot cancel the trip - it would be unfair.

Half an hour into the trip, the kids are bored with the amusements they brought, start fighting in the back of the car and accidentally break a camera. One of the parents shouts, the other tries to concentrate on not missing the next turning. One child needs to go to the restroom, but there isn't a service station. Later there's a traffic jam, and more frustration.

Finally, they reach the leisure park, only to find that a freak power failure has caused its closure for the day. Tired, thoroughly dejected and full of complaint, they console themselves at a fast-food restaurant before starting for home.

Detailed planning based on a bigger picture

Family B's decision to make the trip has come about differently. Hearing of the kids' homework assignment (the same as for Family A), the parents explore with the kids some ideas for an adventure they could write about. After some discussion, they agree on a trip to the leisure park, on the basis that the kids will plan the part of the journey to be taken by road, including two stops for natural breaks and one for light refreshments.

The parents plan the second part of the journey, which will be by rail. They reserve seats to ensure that they enjoy their picnic together on the train. Also, they invite a distant relative who lives near the station to join them for the train journey and the visit to the park. They have been meaning for some time to see this friend - a traveller who has sailed the Atlantic and climbed in the Himalayas, and has plenty of stories to tell.

The journey starts. Having planned the route, the kids are

interested to look out for unusual places or sights, and take notes and photographs for their story. Even if they feel an urge to stop, pride prevents them from requesting a halt until the resting points they planned themselves are reached. If there is a traffic jam, this gives time for extra discussion about the story they will write - and extra time has already been included to compensate for the possibility of such a hold-up. Once on the train, all enjoy the change of transportation and the chance to listen to the friend's adventure stories while enjoying a picnic.

The park is reached - and is closed, due to the same freak power failure that caused disappointment for Family A. How will Family B respond?

Quality of thought influences quality of experience

While, from one point of view, the activity of the two families has been identical - i.e. they have both travelled to the leisure park - their experiences have in reality been of quite different quality. As a result of these differences, their responses to the unexpected closure of the park are significantly contrasting. What for Family A is a disaster is, at worst, a mere inconvenience for Family B. They have created for themselves enjoyable experiences along the way, and are still feeling adventurous!

The kids accumulate data for their story, the parents are glad to spend time with the relative, and all return home satisfied *despite not having achieved their original goal.*

It is not difficult to see from this imaginary example that there is a relationship between the quality of preparation, on the one hand, and the ability to maintain confidence and morale under pressure and adverse conditions, on the other. Yet Family A might justifiably argue that they already know about preparation and planning: they set an objective - to visit the leisure park - and planned the route to achieve it - the car journey.

Two approaches to planning

What is it that makes a higher quality of preparation possible - one that will have a constructive impact on morale? To approach this, we need to examine more closely the differential implied in the example.

Figure 3.4(a) illustrates the level of planning adopted by Family A. An objective is set, and is worked towards over a period of time according to an accustomed method. This might be the case, for example, for a salesperson or sales team working towards a financial target over a month or a quarter. It may also represent a corporate profit target for a year or half-year.

Figure 3.4(b) illustrates the level of preparation adopted by Family B in the example. Instead of focusing all activity on the achievement of a single, finite objective, the activity is seen instead as the medium in which aims can be worked towards.

These aims are not finite, and will continue to be a focus well beyond the timescale of the trip. In the case of Family B, the aims might include providing educational stimuli for the kids and maintaining an active contact with the extended family.

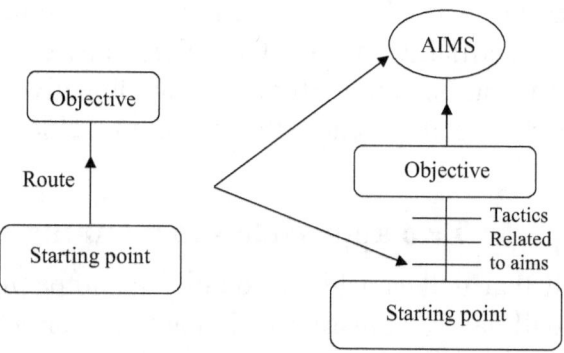

Figure 3.4 Two approaches to planning

Objectives become the concrete steps, often very short term, which serve as benchmarks of progress towards the fulfillment of aims. The larger number of short-term objectives create extra possibilities for achievement and recognition, and consequently for maintaining morale. The implications of this are most important, and relate very closely to current trends in defining and establishing *corporate values* and *quality*.

We shall examine these connections in due course, but first let us be clear about the most important factor which determines whether a parent, a business manager or a government minister plans according to Figure 3.4(a) or Figure 3.4(b). This factor is not to be found in the aims and objectives themselves, nor in the goal nor in the route to it, but in a key difference in thinking.

Two types of thinking

We shall call the type of thinking featured in Family A's planning *route thinking*, and the type of thinking featured in Family B's planning *strategic thinking*. The difference is relative: compared to route thinking, strategic thinking is a response to a higher level of question, and vice versa.

Route thinking limits decision-making permanently to a tactical level: strategic thinking includes the definition of purpose and aim.

Route thinking

The nature of route thinking is well illustrated by the story of the 'Chicken Legs' told by a participant in a leadership seminar. A young, newly married couple sat down to their first Sunday roast. The husband noticed that the legs of the chicken had apparently been cooked separately from the rest of the carcass. The wife confirmed this, saying it was a family tradition and gave a much tastier result - she had learned it from her mother.

A few days later, the husband asks his mother-in-law about this family tradition. She confirms that cutting the legs off before roasting the chicken gives a much better result - she learned it from her mother. Still curious, he telephones the mother-in-law's elderly mother, Agnes, to find out more. Agnes is surprised. 'They're not still cooking chickens like that, are they?' she says. 'I used to cook that way when I first got married, but only because we had such a small oven that you couldn't get a chicken in unless you cut its legs off!'

How much of our personal and communal life is governed by ideas, practices and procedures resembling the 'Chicken Legs' model? If we had the opportunity to replace all the buildings, roads, institutions and man-made objects which currently exist, how many would we keep exactly as they are? However theoretical they may sound, such questions are the life-blood of the strategic thinker. Only through them can vision grow.

Strategic thinking

Strategic thinking addresses the same questions as route thinking from the point of view of a bigger picture and with greater attention to detail.

In the example above, Family B is focused on bigger questions than Family A - how to provide educational stimuli for the kids: how to maintain an active contact with the extended family - *and* on the detail: how many stops to make during the journey, when and what to eat, and so on. Family A is focused only on getting to the leisure park.

The greater vision behind strategic thinking means, first, that Family B is more likely to make full use of a visit to the leisure park and, second, that they are not dependent on it for their 'success'. Route thinking, on the other hand, brings a succession of disappointments for Family A, with a corresponding impact on morale.

Attitudes and Communication

Before we leave the two families, it might be useful to picture how they might view each other's approach. How would Family A, with their route thinking and objective-oriented planning, view and be viewed by Family B, with their larger scale aims and more detailed tactical planning?

We can easily imagine that Family A would be highly critical of Family B, finding them fussy, over-complicated and 'high and mighty'. Unawareness of its own internal action, combined with a 'minus quantity' of vision, automatically yields a negative judgment because Family A's 'rightness' appears threatened.

Family B, on the other hand, might scratch their heads and wonder at Family A's conduct. Able to maintain a positive attitude themselves, Family B might have no impulse to be critical or negative towards Family A. Not having had Family A's experience, however, they might be puzzled and find Family A impossible to understand.

What would be the result if the two families had the opportunity to communicate? It is hard to envisage a full exchange of viewpoints because of the barriers to the growth of vision already mentioned - particularly from the point of view of Family A.

From this, we can start to see something very important about vision.

In many circumstances, Vision is Incommunicable

In many circumstances, vision is incommunicable. We cannot listen without judging, and our judgments, especially under pressure, tend to be made from the level of internal action, attitude or assumption rather than from a fully articulated vision.

And how is a fully articulated vision possible? We articulate in words, yet the realm of vision is beyond words, emerging into verbal formulations only in response to the demands of external situations.

In the era of information technology, computers are said to 'communicate' when a file is merely copied from one terminal to another via a telephone line. Much human communication attempts something similar. If successful, it results in cloning or brainwashing, both of which history proves to be culturally disastrous. If unsuccessful, it takes the form of manipulation or attempted manipulation.

Chief executives often wish that members of the senior management team would 'expand their horizons'. The frustration behind this wish indicates the impossibility of communicating vision. The CEO may suspect that the only solution is for the team's vision to grow. But how will this happen?

Before we approach this, it may be interesting to study an example of a published attempt to communicate organizational vision (see Example 3.1).

Example 3.1

Giro Sport Design: organizational vision (1989)

GUIDING PHILOSOPHY

Values and beliefs

+ Customer satisfaction is first and foremost.
+ It takes great products to be a great company.
+ Integrity is not to be compromised: be honest, consistent and fair.
+ Commitments are made to be fulfilled.
+ Never cut corners; get the details right.
+ The Golden Rule applies to peers, customers, bosses.
+ Teamwork should prevail; think 'we', not 'I'.
+ There is no reason to do any product that is not innovative and high quality.
+ Style is important: all of our products should look great.

Purpose

+ Giro exists to make a positive impact on society---to make people's lives better---through innovative, high-quality products.

TANGIBLE IMAGE

Mission

+ Our mission is to become a great company by the year 2000---to become to the bicycling industry what Nike is to athletic shoes and Apple is to computers.

Vivid description

+ The best riders in the world will be using our products in world-class competition. Winners of the Tour de France, the World Championships and the Olympic Gold Medal will win while wearing Giro helmets. We shall receive unsolicited phone calls and letters from customers who say, 'Thank you for being in business; one of your helmets saved my life.' Our employees will feel that this is the best place they have ever worked. When you ask people to name the top company in the cycling business, the vast majority will say 'Giro'.

Attempts to communicate vision

The closed leader does not attempt to communicate vision, because nothing resembling vision has been articulated. The visionary leader does not attempt to broadcast vision, because in the strategic level of leadership it is known that effective action comes only when people act on the basis of their own growing vision.

Attempts to communicate vision are a feature of the second of the three levels of leadership - the open, or learning level. Those who try to communicate in this way are in the process of learning something.

They are learning, or at least giving themselves the chance to learn, that it can be beneficial to articulate one's own vision. For that is what is happening in the Giro Sport Design example. Perhaps with the help of consultants, and certainly with a substantial investment of time and effort, one (or more) senior person in the organization has taken the trouble to work on expressing his or her own vision, which has probably grown as a consequence.

From the point of view of strategic decision-making, the attempt to foist this onto others is a mistake. But the Giro Sport Design management were, most likely, still learning this. What was there to learn?

The motivational impact of this `vision' on other people is likely, at best, to be short-term and, at worst, to be counter-productive, generating resistance. Such statements may also have an influence on others, who may include the competition, highlighting the areas the company is worried about. For if we are not concerned about them, we probably don't talk about them - just as the aristocracy doesn't talk about money.

The kind of ideas included in Giro Sport Design's statement of organizational vision can be useful in strategic thinking without being brandished in this way. To *publish* a 'vivid description' can create unnecessary risk, for the company may well succeed without any of those things happening, each of which might become a future rod for management's own back.

Generally, the great value of compiling this and similar statements is the effect it has on the vision of those involved in the creation. They will get much more out of compiling such a statement than its recipients ever would - and are usually correspondingly more attached to it. When this is understood, vision has grown.

Searching, and researching, for vision

Is it possible that our modern corporate executives have something to learn from the native American Indian?

This extraordinary race, before the invasions from Europe, numbered some 20 million in the time of Columbus and are now reduced to about 4 million, mostly confined to settlements. They not only inhabited the American continent for at least 28,000 years, but also managed to leave it in at least as good a condition as they found it! We cannot turn back the clock, but can we learn from them?

An important part of native American culture was the Vision Quest. While it may be impossible for us to relate to the experiences connected with this, it may be helpful simply to recall the essence of what was involved.

A Vision Quest was a search for meaning, conducted by young adults and often renewed many times in their life. It could last anything from 4 to 40 days, alone in the wilderness, with little or no food or water. Though conducted in isolation, the Quest constituted one element in life's deeper education, and those embarking on it would receive long and painstaking preparation from one or more elders.

We need vision. This means that we also need to recognize this need. Then we can dedicate time to its growth. This can be a focus for management research in the coming decades, calling in turn for a new way of thinking a way, which promotes strategic questioning, in the meaning we have defined. And through strategic questioning, we may quickly find ways to reveal new areas of relatedness, such as the connection of purpose and aim with responsibility.

CHAPTER 4

Purpose, aim and responsibility

Responsibility as the basis of strategic thinking

We have defined responsibility as the internal limitations on decision-making, and authority as the external limitations on decision-making.

Through the four relationships, which make up the context of management and leadership illustrated in Figure 1.2, we have also uncovered the nature of the relationship between authority and responsibility. This is represented by the Principle of Strategic Responsibility (see Figure 2.5).

How can we link strategic responsibility to the elements of strategic thinking?

This is quite simple. The responsibility upwards, to 'make a full contribution', when made specific to the situation becomes the *purpose*. Similarly, the three remaining strategic responsibilities, towards colleagues, reports and customers/suppliers, are translated into strategic aims specific to the situation (see Figure 4.1).

This convergence of strategic thinking with strategic responsibility gives the foundation for strategic decision-making. First examples have already been given in the Youth Club Holiday illustration in Chapter 2.

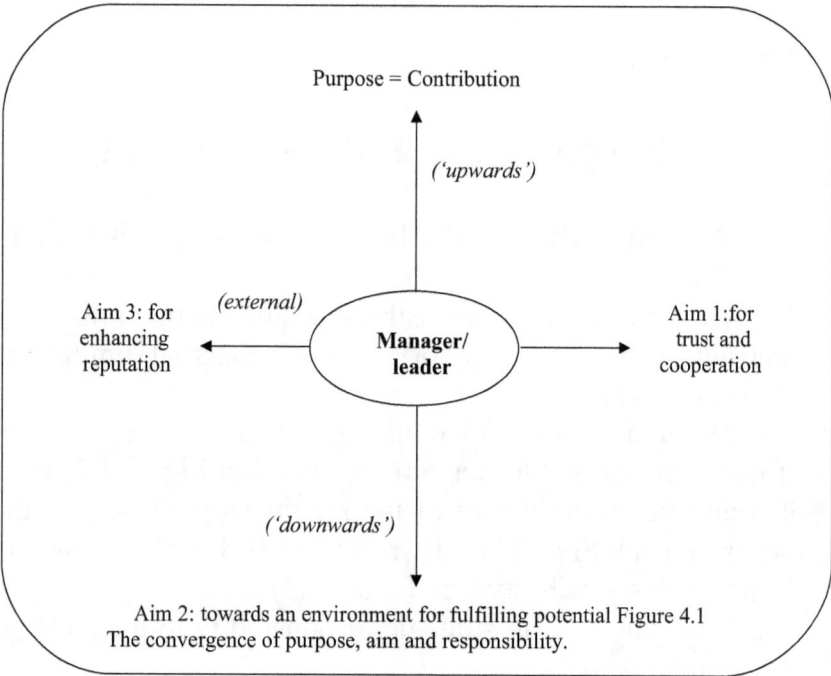

Figure 4.1 The convergence of purpose, aim and responsibility.

Figure 4.1 The convergence of purpose, aim and
responsibility

We shall explore the nature of the connections implicit in this convergence, and then study their application in strategic role definition in Chapter 5.

Three attitudes towards purpose

We have defined purpose as the contribution of a lower authority in relation to a higher authority. Route thinking makes us blind to purpose. As the 'Chicken Legs' story illustrates, we can easily develop habits, which continue to shape our activity despite having lost all connection with the input for the original decision. By contrast, the formulation of purpose can create greater awareness of existing activity.

What, for example, is the purpose of eating? For many people, whether nibbling peanuts in a bar or having a 5-course meal, this question remains unarticulated either before, after or during the entire process. The instinctive mechanisms of the body trigger the appetite, food is somehow available, and both the outer movements of placing the food in the mouth and the inner movements of food towards and within the stomach pass unnoticed. It can all take place while attention is focused on something quite different: a conversation, a book, a train of thought, the television, a football game, another person, and so on.

For an athlete or dancer, eating may have more meaning. For them, eating is very clearly a part of the route towards what they want to achieve. They may aim to reach and maintain a particular body weight or size. Consequently, they will pay attention to details that may appear irrelevant to others: the fat or calorie content of their diet, the timing and frequency of intake, the balance of ingredients over a period, specific changes in the build-up to a competition or performance, and so on.

We can also envisage a third attitude. Imagine someone who develops an active interest in discovering everything possible about her own organism. As part of this, she studies the taste and texture of food. She researches the effects that different combinations and quantities of food have on her sense of vitality. She investigates the different ways in which foods can be produced and prepared, and tries to ascertain through practical experimentation the corresponding influences exerted on the organism.

After a certain period of theoretical and practical research, our imaginary student has a different understanding of eating. Based on this understanding, a new vision can be articulated. This may contain two elements: a statement of how the environment of the activity of eating is understood, and a statement of the student's personal attitude towards this understanding.

In this case, vision might be articulated as follows: 'The quality of my organism depends, at least in part, on the type of food it receives, and on the way food is digested. I am responsible for this, in respect of my own organism.'

Based on this vision, our researcher might now define the purpose of eating as: 'to provide a source of energy for sustaining and developing the physical, mental and emotional life of the organism'.

Before we trace the possible further development of the researcher's strategy, let us clarify one aspect of the contrast between these three approaches to purpose. This is that the second approach will gain at least as much as the first, and probably more, and the third approach will gain at least as much as the second, and probably more.

Example 4.1
A researcher's strategy for eating

VISION

'The health of my organism depends, at least in part, on the type of food it receives, and on the way food is digested. I am responsible for this, in relation to my own organism.'

MISSION

To provide a source of energy for sustaining and developing the physical, mental and emotional life of the organism.

STRATEGIC AIMS

1. Locate a selection of suitable sources of food.
2. Secure a range of reliable environments for the preparation and consumption of food.
3. Develop additional means of research.

OBJECTIVES

This week:
1. Find 2 butchers, 2 vegetable stores and 2 dairy food stores whose stock meets the criteria of the Research *(Aim 1)*.
2. Agree delivery arrangements with these suppliers for regular items (*Aim 1)*.

3. Establish suppliers' criteria for discounts on possible future bulk orders *(Aim 1)*.
4. Also by the end of next week, find 5 restaurants within a 5-mile radius, which serve food which meets the research criteria *(Aim 2)*.

By the end of next week:
5. Buy an oven suitable for baking bread *(Aim 2)*.
6. Find 5 friends who wish to explore and enjoy new dishes and are ready to make their own facilities available *(Aim 2)*.
7. Create a reading plan for next month *(Aim 3)*.

Within the next 2 months:
8. Find 3 friends who would like to research together on this subject *(Aim 3)*.
9. Compile a list of grants available for research into food, eating and digestion *(Aim 3)*.

TACTICS

Day 1: Phone to establish lists of butchers, veg. and dairy stores, restaurants, friends to visit and sources of ovens *(Objectives 1, 4, 5, 6, 8)*.

Days 2 and 3 : Visits *(Objectives 1, 4, 5, 6, 8)*.

Day 4: am: review of best possibilities *(Objectives 1, 4, 5, 6, 8)*; pm: phone more friends *(Objectives 6, 8)*.

Day 5: am: second visits to secure supplies *(Objectives 1, 2, 3, 4, 6)*; pm: buy oven *(Objective 5)*, and have some time off!

The first approach, a reaction to instinct, achieves the

activity of eating. The second includes this activity in the achievement of an objective - a particular measurement. The third has the chance to achieve much more. As long as the vision and purpose are adhered to, the activity of eating may continue to provide a medium for improvement. The objective-related improvement of the dancer or athlete may stop once the objective is reached; our researcher may be free of that danger.

Responding to the question: 'Why?'

How will our three types of eater respond if we ask them why they are eating as they do? We can imagine that the first type of eater, who has never defined a purpose for eating, might respond at first humorously and then, if the questioning persists, dismissively or even angrily.

The athlete and ballet dancer would be able to explain their planned approach - very likely with less emotion and without feeling attacked. The researcher would be able to give a much fuller response, and perhaps even engage the questioner in a wider discussion on the whole subject.

What about ourselves? How are we able to respond when someone asks why we do something in a certain way, *why* we have a certain habit, why we work in the occupation we do? At what point do we start to become defensive, irritable - even aggressive? The existence of that point can indicate where there is an opportunity for vision to grow, perhaps for new purpose and meaning to be found.

These three attitudes we have addressed - which we might call reactive, objective-driven and research-led - correspond directly to the existence of the three levels of leadership whose nature we have studied in Chapter 2.

What is significant from the point of view of language is the use of the term *strategy*. In many organizations, the word strategy is used in a way which corresponds to the athlete's plan for reaching the objective for weight control. In other words, an objective is set - perhaps a financial one - and the plan to achieve it is given the name strategy.

In Leadership Level 3, the plan to achieve an objective is called tactics, and strategy - the conscious translation of vision into action - encompasses the whole process, starting with the articulation of vision.

In strategic decision-making there is therefore a greater number of steps, and purpose is defined *before* objectives. *Strategic aims* come as the vitally important link in the hierarchy between purpose and objectives.

Creating strategic aims

Strategic aims have to be created. They can be the most difficult part of strategic thinking in which to develop expertise. When well formulated, they can become the means for including values and quality improvements in strategy.

We have already defined strategic aims as signposts for action to fulfill the purpose. Research and experience indicate that the ideal number of strategic aims is three. At the same time, the strategic decision-maker must be satisfied that the three aims encompass all requirements for fulfilling the purpose, at least over a certain timescale.

Let us pursue the formulation of a strategy for eating! The purpose, or mission, has been formulated as: 'to provide an inflow of energy for sustaining and developing the physical, mental and emotional life of the organism'.

What are the three aims - signposts for action - that can give rise to action likely to secure the purpose? Our researcher might think these through as follows. First there will need to be a range of reliable sources for the types of food, which have already been shown to be beneficial. A range - because it may be unwise to rely on a single source.

Second, the research may have shown that certain environments are more conducive to the stated purpose than others. Third, the research cannot be regarded as complete; it needs to be extended, possibly shared with others and one day, perhaps, be published.

The researcher therefore formulates the three strategic aims thus: first, to secure a range of reliable sources of food; second, to locate a selection of suitable environments for the preparation and consumption of food; third, to develop additional means of research.

After further pondering, the researcher is satisfied that the purpose will be met as long as these three aims are achieved, bearing in mind that, at that point, new aims may be needed.

The art of non-numerical objective-setting

How to achieve the aims? Now that purpose has been split into aims, the next step is to establish objectives. In strategic decision-making, *objectives* are defined as *concrete measures of productivity in relation to aim*. Concrete means *quantified and measurable in time*. 'I'm going to reduce my golf handicap' expresses an aim. 'Two strokes off my handicap by the end of next month' is an objective.

Research indicates that managers find difficulty in setting concrete objectives which are not financial. What are generally proposed as objectives either have the non-concrete form appropriate to an aim - but lack a strategic aim's link to purpose - or are financial measures to be achieved. Their limitations, and the value of well-constructed non-financial objectives, may become clearer if we pursue the golf handicap analogy.

A golfer wishes to reduce his handicap. This is an aim - possibly strategic. He sets himself an objective of 'two strokes off the handicap by the end of next month'. How will he go about this? The formulation of the objectives will not necessarily bring about the action that will create the changes he is looking for.

For example, he may continue to play twice a week, keeping his objective in mind continually. Every time he plays a poor shot, misses a putt or slices a drive, this will be interpreted as a failure in relation to his objective. Perhaps he will start walking harder, swinging faster, swearing louder - and later complain to colleagues in the clubhouse about what went wrong.

The objective the golfer has set corresponds to the type of financial objectives often set by and for management and sales teams. They rigorously monitor costs and sales figures, blowing hot and cold exhorting and chastising each other as the target date approaches - without affecting the outcome as strongly as they could. With less route thinking, and more strategic thinking, a great deal more could be achieved.

From the point of view of the golfer, non-numerical objectives, nonetheless concrete, could be much more useful. The possibility of his creating them depends largely on what he can see about his own game. Perhaps he tends to leave his approach shots short of the green. A productive objective might be to play a round with the aim of playing *beyond* the target green on every hole for the first nine holes. In this way, he might find out what is producing the mistake, and find a way of curing it.

Alternatively, he finds that he often slices his drives. He sets himself the following objective: 'within two weeks to be able to slice or hook the ball deliberately'. As tactics towards this, he engages the local professional to help him master the adaptations of golf swing required to achieve his objective.

Through developing and working towards these two non-numerical objectives - playing through the green on a series of holes, and learning to be able to hook or slice deliberately - the golfer probably has a better chance of gaining control, and therefore of lowering his handicap, than by occupying his mind with 'two strokes off!' Maybe he will reduce the handicap by more than two strokes!

Initiatives to instill values and quality

The parallel opportunities that exist in business for working with non-financial objectives are generally overlooked. Why should this be so? Why should the focus be on finance? The answer lies in the preponderance of route thinking. Financial measures are the 'lowest common denominator' in business, the most easily accessible form of control - or at least of apparent control.

Non-financial objectives require greater vision before they can come into existence, because as a general rule they are unique to each business situation. They may even need to be uniquely adapted to the outlook and relative strengths of the executives involved. The barriers to their creation are essentially those set out in Chapter 3 under 'Barriers to the growth of vision'.

It is generally found that, when organizations opt for an externally sourced initiative based around the topic of 'values' or 'quality', there has been an absence, or virtual absence, of non-financial objective-setting over an extended period of time prior to the decision for the initiative.

Relating objectives to strategic aim

To complete our imaginary researcher's strategy for eating, we shall develop objectives relating to the strategic aims already created. The first aim was to secure a range of reliable sources of food. What will be the *concrete measures of productivity* in relation to this aim?

Three is generally found to be a good number of objectives in relation to an aim, so we shall formulate three - all to be secured within one week: first, to find two butchers, two vegetable stores and two dairy food suppliers whose stock meets the criteria of the research; second, to agree delivery arrangements with these suppliers for regular items; and third, to establish the suppliers' criteria for discounts on possible future bulk orders.

The second aim was defined as 'to locate a selection of suitable environments for the preparation and consumption of food'. Three objectives towards this - also to be secured within one week -   could be as follows.

First, to find five friends who wish to explore and enjoy eating new dishes and are ready to make their own kitchens and dining rooms available; second, to buy an oven suitable for baking bread; and, third, to find three restaurants within a 5-mile radius which serve food that satisfies the research criteria.

The third aim was 'to develop additional means of research'. The first objective for this could be to create, within a fortnight, a reading plan for the following month. Others could be, within the next two months, to find three friends who would like to research together around this subject, and to compile a list of grants available for research into the science of food and digestion.

The important item is the structure of thinking that enables three aims, which are not concrete, to be translated into a set of nine concrete objectives that will provide measures to indicate progress.

As these objectives near completion, at various intervals in the coming months, others can be substituted in accordance with the new conditions that arise. Eventually, at least one of the aims will need to be replaced, since it will have become part of the researcher's routine and will no longer require attention.

Tactics = The Application of Resources

When objectives are in place, the final step is to develop *tactics*. In strategic decision-making, tactics are defined as *the application of resources to secure the objective*. In the case of our imaginary researcher developing a strategy for eating, the main resource which needs to be applied for securing these first objectives is the researcher's own *time*.

Taking the three objectives for securing the first aim, we may envisage the following tactics. The first day will be invested in making telephone calls to establish lists of butchers, vegetable stores, dairy food suppliers, restaurants and friends to visit. Also, perhaps, to find a source for the oven purchase. Days 2 and 3 might be devoted to visiting those listed.

The morning of Day 4 will be used to review the most favourable options, to be followed by second visits in the afternoon to secure the food sources and to buy the oven. The morning of Day 5 presents an opportunity to telephone more friends in connection with aims 2 and 3, and maybe to bake some bread. In the afternoon? Some time off (for a round of golf?)!

Tactics can be similarly developed for the remaining objectives. Built into the tactics will be time for reviewing the objectives and, in due course, the aims. The whole structure, from the articulation of vision to the planning of tactical action, constitutes our researcher's strategy for eating (see Example 4.1).

Differentiating between route and strategic thinking

The structure of strategic thinking illustrated above has important properties which can have a significant impact on both decision-making and communication. The degree to which this structure is characteristic of the thinking *throughout* an organization will play a large part in determining the quality of corporate culture.

The properties of strategic thinking include contrasts, some of them very subtle, with conventional formulations of, for example, mission and objectives. It will be useful to be as clear as possible about these differences before we go further.

In Example 4.2, examples of actual corporate mission statements are shown, reproduced from annual reports. From the point of view of strategic decision-making, these show different levels of thinking, which to the practiced eye also says a great deal about the quality of thinking that is likely to exist in the respective organizations.

Mission, or purpose, is defined as *the contribution of a lower authority in relation to a higher authority*. Generally speaking, from the point of view of a business organization, the higher authority is its marketplace. When the marketplace decides that the organization can no longer contribute, then the organization will decay. It is therefore important for the organization to define and to be able to express its contribution.

Confusion between Mission and Aim

The stated mission of McCormick & Company does not constitute a mission from the point of view of Leadership Level 3. This is because it fails to define the contribution of the organization within its environment.

What is stated looks at first sight like an aim - to expand - though really it is an objective simply lacking the basic measures of turnover, profit or market share. Its woolliness is exacerbated by the use of the word primary, which suggests secondary, tertiary and so on. Why not create a single well-formulated one!

The answer may well be that its senior managers cannot do that, because they are not addressing the question that would help to produce a genuine mission statement. It may easily happen in a successful company that, after a generation or two, managers and shareholders become more concerned with how to grow than with how to contribute. This can be the start of the company's downfall. For a considerable time, it can continue to flourish, largely as the result of the momentum created in the past by people who may no longer be around.

Example 4.2
A cross-section of corporate mission statements
(*Source:* Annual Reports)

McCORMICK & COMPANY
The primary mission of McCormick & Company is to expand our worldwide leadership position in the spice, seasoning and flavouring markets.

THE SATURN DIVISION OF GENERAL MOTORS
To market vehicles developed and manufactured in the United States that are world leaders in quality, cost, and customer satisfaction through the integration of people, technology and business systems and to transfer knowledge, technology, and experience throughout General Motors.

PUBLIC SERVICE COMPANY OF NEW MEXICO
Our mission is to work for the success of the people we serve by providing our CUSTOMERS reliable electric service, energy information, and energy options that best satisfy their needs.

DELUXE CHECKS

The mission of Deluxe Checks is to provide all banks, S&Ls, and investment firms with error-free financial instruments delivered in a timely fashion.

OTIS ELEVATOR
Our mission is to provide any customer a means of moving people and things up, down and sideways over short distances with higher reliability than any other similar enterprise in the world.

AMERICAN RED CROSS
The mission of the American Red Cross is to improve the quality of human life; to enhance self-reliance and concern for others; and to help people avoid, prepare for and cope with emergencies.

HEWLETT-PACKARD COMPANY
Hewlett-Packard is a major designer and manufacturer of electronic products and systems for measurement and computation. HP's basic business purpose is to provide the capabilities and services needed to help customers worldwide improve their personal and business effectiveness.

When questions such as 'how to grow?' leave their rightful place - at the level of strategic aim - and usurp the place of purpose, then decay is setting in. The degeneration of strategic thinking into route thinking is a clear sign of such decay.

The stated mission of The Saturn Division of General Motors contains a mixture of hype and platitude that is enough to run rings round anybody! The formulation results in a sentence that would hardly trip off the tongue in conversation.

It is not clear who the customers are or what the contribution is, and the mistake is made, from the word `through' onwards, of including aspects that would be better formulated as strategic aims.

One can picture the senior management team discussing for hours the inclusion of this word or that in this statement - perhaps with a 'mission statements manual' to hand! All to no avail, if the real sense of contribution cannot be separated from bravado.

The stated mission of the Public Services Company of New Mexico points more towards a contribution, if rather vaguely.

This is a customer-oriented organization, putting the word CUSTOMERS in big letters! There may be too many customers to list, or the business may be too diverse.

The use of the word customer bears comparison with the use of financial objectives: a kind of lowest common denominator. The frequency of the word in this selection of mission statements calls to mind the case of British Rail who, as part of a customer-orientation culture shift, stopped calling their customers passengers and started calling them customers. But how do their customers see themselves? Surely as travellers, or passengers, while they are using a train! In this respect, British Rail may have had a better formulation before money was spent on finding a new one!

The mission of Deluxe Checks says who its customers are. From the point of view of strategic decision-making, there are two elements which reduce its usefulness as a basis for planning. First, the inclusion of the qualifiers 'error-free' and 'in a timely fashion'.

Open to public view, such terms may be interpreted as management's view of the firm's existing or potential weaknesses - areas to be improved. These may be better expressed as strategic aims, quickly translated into objectives and made routine. Real quality services and products, like Swiss watches, don't need such window-dressing as part of a mission statement.

Second, the word 'all' single-handedly reduces this formulation to near-objective, i.e. concrete, status. It may also raise a question of credibility: all banks, etc., worldwide? Is the strategy really based on that? Or is it boardroom bravado? What is wrong with: 'The mission of Deluxe Checks is to provide financial instruments for banks, S&Ls and investment firms'?

Otis Elevator's stated mission has the advantage of not confining itself to a particular product, or route. The disadvantage is the unnecessary comparison with other enterprises. Being better than anybody else will not necessarily satisfy customers: the competition may also be uninteresting! And there may be other enterprises that have great reliability but, for other reasons, remain unattractive to customers. At best, this again should be demoted to strategic aim level. Mission is for what is most *permanent* in the organization's relationship with its market.

The American Red Cross expresses this well in the first part of its mission statement: the remainder, from the point of view of strategic decision-making, consists of strategic aims.

The stated mission of Hewlett-Packard gives the best illustration of strategic thinking in this selection. The first part is really closer to being part of vision. The second part is the mission.

Confusion between objective and aim

Turning to the corporate objectives listed in Example 4.3, we shall again see differences between the type of objectives that may get published in annual reports and those that are useful from the point of view of decision-making and communication in strategic decision-making.

Almost without exception, the stated objectives are not concrete. The few that are (the last five McCormick & Co. objectives), are at 'lowest common denominator' level - that is, they are financial objectives. The remainder have the non-concrete property typical of aims, without having the signpost quality typical of strategic aims in strategic decision-making.

The six Nike objectives could be more productively stated as three strategic aims, each supported by concrete objectives. They could be, for example, as follows. The first aim is to build on the strength of the existing athletic brand. Objectives for core businesses and new businesses can be developed in relation to this aim.

The second aim could be to develop new product lines in growing markets. Objectives for this can be developed in relation to the markets for fitness, women's products and mature Americans. The third aim is to increase margins. This will require objectives relating to inventory management and product stream-lining.

La-Z-Boy's stated objectives are also aims. The first two are useful, the third and fourth could be merged, and the fifth can be eliminated, since it depends in any case on the achievement of the others. This would leave three strategic aims, from which concrete objectives could be developed.

The Owens-Corning stated objectives are again aims, and are fine in this capacity as far as they go. They could go much further, for they contain nothing demonstrably specific to the organization, and their usefulness in planning is very limited because they communicate little, if anything at all, by way of signpost. Just textbook clichés!

Example 4.3
A cross-section of corporate objectives
(Source: Annual Reports)

McCormick & Company's Objectives (as stated in 1990)
1. Improve the returns from each of our existing operating groups---consumer, industrial, food, service, international, and packaging.
2. Dispose of those parts of our business which do not or cannot generate adequate returns or do not fit with our business strategy.
3. Make selective acquisitions which complement our current businesses and can enhance our overall returns.
4. Achieve a 20 per cent return on equity.
5. Achieve a net sales growth rate of 10 per cent per year.
6. Maintain an average earnings per share growth rate of 15 per cent per year.
7. Maintain total debt to total capital at 40 per cent or less.
8. Pay out 25 per cent to 35 per cent of net income in dividends.

Nike's objectives (as stated in 1987)
1. Protect and improve NIKE's position as the number one athletic brand in America, with particular attention to the

company's existing core businesses in running, basketball, tennis, football, baseball, and kid's shoes and newer businesses with good potential like golf and soccer.

2. Build a strong momentum in the growing fitness market, beginning with walking, workout and cycling.
3. Intensify the company's effort to develop products that women need and want.
4. Explore the market for products specifically designed for the requirements of maturing Americans.
5. Direct and manage the company's international business as it continues to develop.
6. Continue the drive for increased margins through proper inventory management and fewer, better products.

La-Z-Boy's objectives (as stated in 1990)
1. To position La-Z-Boy as a full-time furniture manufacturer.
2. To strengthen La-Z-Boy's brand name image with American families and business people.
3. To improve the quality of the company's distribution network.
4. To expand production capacity and make it more efficient.
5. To continue to gain financial strength.

Owens-Corning's objectives (as stated in 1990)
1. To anticipate our customers' requirements and provide them with the products which meet their market, quality and service needs.
2. To maintain our number one market positions through

continued leadership in technology, manufacturing, and marketing.

3. To maximize cash flow for continued debt reduction.
4. To focus on operating profit improvements through productivity programmes and focused market development.
5. To make the most of the talents of our people and provide them with the opportunity and training to reach their full potential.

The first three of the McCormick & Company's stated objectives are actually aims: the remaining five are objectives which will be the concrete measures of productivity in relation to the aims. The formulation is fine given the reservations expressed above about the mission statement shown in Example 4.2. The underlying problem could be one of spirit: Where is the real growth? No doubt the stockholders will be happy with the payout. The question is: Where is the organization going long term? These strategic statements raise doubts as to whether anyone is thinking about such a question.

Strategic Thinking and the Human Resource

We've explored strategic thinking and its application in defining and expressing the purpose, intent and performance measurement of a whole organization. How can this quality of thinking be applied to the way jobs and roles are defined within the organization?

We are now ready to investigate the art and science of strategic role definition.

CHAPTER 5

Strategic Role Definition and the Use of Time

The role definition in corporate strategy

We saw in Chapter 1 that strategic decision-making requires an awareness of strategy on three levels. This applies also in the creation of a strategic role definition.

First, there must be an awareness of strategic elements of the context. This may be part of the corporate strategy or specific elements, such as aims or objectives, of a senior manager - a higher level of authority.

Second, there must be a full strategy, including vision, purpose, strategic aims, objectives and tactics, for the fulfillment of the role. Third, there must be strategic awareness at the tactical level, the level of activity.

The strategic role definition proves the existence of these three levels of strategic awareness, welding together the strategic elements of the context, the strategy for the role itself and, within that, the strategy for developing tactical ability.

When everyone in an organization acts on the basis of a strategic role definition, the organization is strategic. Its culture is such that the time usage of every individual and group is directly related to corporate strategy. The idea of such a culture can provide a development aim for many organizations.

A definition encompassing authority and responsibility

Where route thinking breeds complexity, strategic thinking creates simplicity. Where route thinking leads to divisions and fragmentation, strategic thinking builds connections and unity. Where route thinking may need ten pieces of paper, strategic thinking may need only one, if any.

How, then, do these two approaches relate to the allocation of jobs and the organization of the human resource'? To find a clear definition of a management role is not an easy task. As we saw in Chapter 1, management itself is the conduct of the relationship between authority and responsibility, both of which may change.

If a management role is not to stagnate, there must be room within it to allow for responsibility to grow and authority to increase. Also, growth of responsibility and increase in authority may not be simultaneous. How can all this be embraced in the definition of a job?

Route thinking cannot handle this question. It may not be able to conceive of the existence of the question. For this reason, the full definition of a job does not exist in many organizations. In general, insofar as the question of defining jobs is addressed, there exists a fragmented approach, which at best adds up to a *description*.

Route thinking and job description

There may be a contract for the job. This is unlikely to need or to benefit from frequent reference to it. It will lay down the parameters of the relationship between employer and employee, generally in the form of *lowest common denominators*. It will state what is demanded, in terms of such aspects as the amount of time spent at work, and possibly certain basic aspects of good conduct.

The contract may also state what is forbidden - normally in terms of what is forbidden to everybody in a similar environment or position. It may also indicate what is permitted in terms of time off, sick and maternity/paternity allowance, and what is required from each side in order to terminate the arrangement. Most likely the financial arrangements will be included, together with any arrangements for reviewing them.

The contract is in many cases extended by a series of responses to 'What if . . . ?' questions. These clauses, representing rich pickings for the legal profession, are apparently geared to enumerating all the possible eventualities that might cause future difficulties or antipathy between the parties, and to providing advance solutions of greater, or usually lesser, concreteness.

Tactics: the focus of route thinking

Either as part of the contract or separately, there may also be a job description. It is important to realize that, in most cases, the job description defines activity. We shall define activity as the action produced by route thinking. This means that, from the point of view of strategic thinking, the conventional job description addresses only tactics. This has two consequences of particular importance in the life and development of organizations.

The first is that, by addressing activity, the job description builds in limitations to the growth of responsibility and authority, because of its habit-driven nature. The second is that the ability of the organization as a whole to respond strategically to change within its environment is severely handicapped. The dominance of activity, without regularly addressing and incorporating internal action, results in a rigidity that can spell a death sentence for the organization.

A further implication of this descriptive approach is that any new development plan within the role, or the written consequences of a disciplinary meeting, results in additional pieces of paper - additional fragments which, when added to all the others, still fail to give a clear indication of the precise contribution to be made or of the measures of effectiveness and quality of performance.

Strategic thinking and role definition

In Chapter 1, we explored the criteria for definitions for strategic thinking and decision-making. The same criteria can be put to good use in defining roles. Using the language we have developed for strategic decision-making, it is possible to transform the job descriptions produced by route thinking into role definitions, which satisfy these criteria.

Translated into the context of jobs, the principal criteria for definitions in strategic decision-making are as follows. First, the role definition must distinguish between what is relatively permanent and what is relatively short-term or flexible within the role.   Second, the role definition needs to be useful as a reference point for decision-making on both current and future issues. Third, it needs to clarify the key relationships that will be developed in the defined role.

A legal case

To illustrate the development opportunity afforded by the transition from job description to role definition, we shall study two examples, one at senior and one at junior level, generated during a development project undertaken by a London law firm.

The firm was in the process of completing the transition from being a relatively small, traditional practice centered around long-established private client and matrimonial departments to becoming a fully-fledged city law firm specializing in corporate and commercial work.

Reproduced in Example 5.1 is a description of the duties of the managing partner of the firm at the start of the transition. It comprises mainly a list of activities, with all the limitations and dangers for the organization that have already been indicated above. In items, which contain something other than a reference to, or description of, activity, the language is generally too woolly to be of practical use or significance.

Example 5.1

Duties of the managing partner

The managing partner is the chief executive of the firm, accountable to the partnership. The managing partner is the central figure responsible for overseeing the business management of the firm, though he must delegate authority to other partners and administrative staff where appropriate.

1. Anticipate and analyse problems for the firm, developing the means to resolve or prevent those problems.
2. Always act in the best interests of the firm by putting the firm ahead of any partner's personal interests.
3. Monitor and assess the organizational structure of the firm, recommending or implementing changes as necessary to ensure its effective operation.
4. Maintain a high profile in every office, and be available to all people in the firm (though ensuring that all matters are first referred to the appropriate individuals before becoming personally involved).
5. Ensure that all partnership and management decisions are implemented on a timely basis and in the manner prescribed.
6. Serve on the Executive Board and the Partnership Committee.
7. Administer the profit-sharing system and supervise profit distribution.
8. Liaise and work closely with the chairman, the heads of department and the admin. partners.
9. Be responsible for supervising the finance director. In

particular, although all administrative decisions are the immediate responsibility of the finance director, the managing partner bears ultimate responsibility for those decisions and provides the authority for issues outside the scope of the finance director's job description, and it is to him that the office administrator, marketing manager and director of studies are answerable.

10. Be responsible for all personnel matters including training and evaluation.

11. Undertake such other duties as the partners shall delegate.

Example 5.2 shows the role definition created as part of the development process. Unlike its predecessor, it meets the criteria of strategic decision-making defined above. By using elements of the language of the third level of leadership - vision, purpose, strategic aims, objectives and tactics - a clear distinction is created between what is relatively permanent, expressed in the vision and mission, what is relatively short-term, expressed by the objectives, the links between the two, represented by the strategic aims, and the short-term action, represented by the tactics.

Example 5.2
The managing partner: strategic role definition

VISION
The partnership, in servicing its clients, requires its commercial and organizational development to be actively controlled. The managing partner will have the authority, and be responsible, for such control.

PURPOSE
Secure the partnership's future commercial and organizational health.

AIMS
1. Establish throughout the partnership agreed principles of evaluating and improving the all-round performance of partners, associates and staff.
2. Instil and develop financial controls which will secure the long-term interests of partners.
3. Represent the interests of the partners, as owners, to the senior executives of the firm, and vice versa.

OBJECTIVES
1. Develop role definition at senior levels by the end of month 3.
2. Institute performance appraisal and development at senior levels by the end of month 6.
3. Establish flexible policies on partner recruitment and development by the end of month 9.
4. Establish profit centers with full authority for own budget, by the end of month 3.

133

5. Agree commercially sound policies on profit distribution by the end of month 3.
6. Define and secure overdraft reduction plan with bankers by the end of month 3.
7. Develop with the heads of department a 1-year practice development strategy and gain approval from the partners by the end of month 3.
8. Agree with partners the criteria for interim reports, by the end of month 3.
9. Secure the renewed support of partners at quarterly intervals.

TACTICS
1. For objectives 1 and 2: facilitation by an external specialist.
2. Objectives 3, 4, 5 and 7 to be agenda items for the heads of department.
3. Communicate plan for objective 6 as basis of HoDs' planning.
4. Prepare presentations for objectives 8 and 9.

One of the interesting points about a role definition such as this is that the entire role as formulated may have only a short duration, because the speed of transformation of the organization as a whole can be such that the formulation of vision and purpose may well change within, say, a 12-month period.

At the end of such a period, it may no longer be the case, for example, that the full weight of commercial and organizational development will fall on the shoulders of a single person. Once the current objectives of the managing partner have been achieved, the organization as a whole will understand more about these questions, and know what action is necessary to secure the firm's future commercial and organizational health.

At that point, responsibility for these areas can be more widely shared, and the managing partner's role may develop further - perhaps as a figurehead with time and energy to devote more attention to the representation of the firm in its marketplace.

The role definition as strategy

Thus the role definition can become a living, growing reference point for decision-making and time management. The tactics already generated in Example 5.2 dictate time usage. For the strategy to be implemented, personal influence is required, which will need the vehicle of meetings and the setting aside of time for thorough preparation.

When regularly updated through a well-managed performance appraisal process, the role definition can also become a concise and clear basis for personal development. When added to a suitably worded covering letter, it can even replace all other documentation concerning employment. In this way, it becomes an important medium - perhaps the most important - through which the strategic development of the organization can be made secure.

Examples 5.3 and 5.4 may give a fuller insight into how this might be possible. These present a role definition for an administrative assistant who, prior to the said development project, had no documentation relating to her job other than a standard, rather long-winded contract.

The combination of the strategic definition of the role, plus the covering letter confirming general details of employment, provides a permanently renewable focus for the effective conduct and development of her contribution.

Example 5.3
Strategic role definition (administrative support)
Date: .
NAME:
Address:

Dear

TERMS OF EMPLOYMENT
It is a pleasure to welcome you to your new career with XYZ Inc. This is to confirm the arrangements agreed between us, as follows:

1. That from today's date you will work to help promote the interests of XYZ, according to the attached job definition.
2. That the job, as defined, will be carried out in a way which creates a good impression within the firm and among clients. Training and informal help will be given for this. In the event of any uncertainty in this area, it is up to you to ask for assistance or advice.
3. That during (and after any termination of) employment with XYZ, you will respect the privileged access given you to details of the company's business, acknowledging that such access is given solely for the purpose of fulfilling your role within XYZ.
4. That remuneration will be by monthly salary together with such holiday, bonus, pension and other arrangements as may be agreed between us from time to time relative to the contribution made (details to be listed

in the job definition), that this contract may be terminated by either party with a minimum of two months' notice, and that statutory sickness arrangements apply.

5. That the details of the attached job definition will be reviewed and updated, with your participation, at 6-monthly intervals, the most recent job definition forming the remainder of this contract.

Wishing you a rewarding career with XYZ.
Yours sincerely
Terms Agreed:

....

DIRECTOR   EMPLOYEE

Terms of Employment (*contd*)
ROLE DEFINITION:

[Name]

Purpose
To provide an administrative support service for three of the Firm's partners: Mr A, Ms B and Mrs C.
Aims
- To produce and distribute outgoing documents reliably and accurately.
- To control the collection of payments from clients.
- To provide a friendly and efficient reception service for visitors and for incoming telephone calls and mail.

Objectives
1. Draft letters and enclosures received for word processing

to be despatched within 24 hours, free of errors in typography and layout.

2. Copies of all outgoing mail to be collated and passed to [Name] at the end of each week.

3. All clients to be billed monthly on the basis of partners' timesheets and/or specific instructions: payment to be received within an average of 45 days.

4. Incoming mail to be distributed by 0930 each day: incoming phone calls to be answered within 4 rings between 0830 and 1730 Monday to Friday: adequate cover to be arranged by you if unavailable for this.

5. Availability of all office supplies to be maintained through your own stock plan, communicated monthly to [Name] and within agreed budgets.

6. All work to be completed between 0830 and 1730 Monday to Friday.

Remuneration
- Salary: x per annum, paid monthly in arrears
- Holidays: y days per annum, plus public holidays--- timings to be dovetailed with those of colleagues in order to protect the smooth running of XYZ services (one month's notice for any holiday period exceeding 2 days).

Role definition agreed:

....

[Name]   Director

Many organizations have had the experience of investing large amounts of cash, or senior management time, or both, in the development of strategies which, for all their excellence and appropriateness for the organization in its marketplace, could not be implemented.

The principal reason for this inability to implement new strategic ideas has been the inflexibility of the workforce as a whole to adapt its activity and its thinking. The way in which roles are defined can play a vital part in creating the flexibility needed for an organization to stay healthy and receptive.

Time: the third level of strategic awareness

The creation of strategic role definitions at all levels of the organization is a sure sign of efforts to change the direction of thinking from route to strategic thinking. At the same time, a further development, dependent on each individual, is needed if the organization's future strategy is to become fully realized. This is based on a new attitude towards time.

Time usage and time management

How do we decide how to use our time? We all know, theoretically at least, that our life is finite in time, as well as in space. Does this knowledge affect our use of it? Or do we conveniently forget our mortality, and leave the noble changes till `later'?

To address these questions, it can be helpful to distinguish time usage from time management. Time management will include how we control the investment of time once its use has been decided.

Time usage will include the process through which we decide how to invest time in the first place.

The value of time

Perhaps we are influenced by the fact that the exact time limits of our life are unknown. Suppose we knew now the exact time, day and year of our own death. Would this knowledge make a difference to our thinking, to our decision-making, and therefore to our use of time?

So easily we overlook the fact that time is our most precious resource. It is more precious, for example, than money - because it is more finite and uniquely ours. How much would you have to be paid in order to sacrifice, say, five years of healthy life? What would you be ready to give in order to receive an extra five years of healthy life?

Certainly, we could begin to practice a more strategic approach to the application of this most precious resource by considering the next six months. How many days are in that period? How can they be spent? We know for certain, i.e. assuming we remain alive through those six months, that those days will be spent! On what is this based? The legacy of habit? The dictates of an objective to be achieved? The habitual demands of others? A decision made long ago, and now automatic?

Time is a tactical resource

We have already seen that, from the point of view of strategic decision-making, the use of time is part of tactics. Its quality will therefore always depend on the quality of thinking and decision-making preceding it.

For many people, there is no higher level of thinking than tactics, which are therefore haphazard because there is no direction. For others, time usage results from strategic thinking, and a portion of available time is always allocated for the further expansion of vision. Most of us, perhaps, are somewhere in the middle.

How can we be more certain that our allocation and usage of time are of good quality? This question can become a central component of the process of strategic questioning on which the growth of our vision depends. And there may be a great deal to learn about the reality of our experience of time.

The experience of time

A closer inspection of our experience of time can reveal extraordinary insights. Take, for example, an apparently objective period of time: the duration of a soccer match. Forty-five minutes for each half, and a 15-minute interval: in total: 1 hour 45 minutes. This period of time can be experienced quite differently, in terms of its *apparent* duration, by different people.

For the regular supporter, eager to see his side win this tightly contested game against traditional rivals and thus still be in with a chance of winning this season's championship, the first half is over very quickly. For his new girlfriend, who has never been to a soccer match before, hates large crowds and was bitterly cold to start with, the whole business is an endless nightmare. At the end of the tedious first half, which seemed to take an eternity, and with all the shouting around her almost bursting her eardrums, she finds it difficult to believe there is still more to come!

An awareness of the reality of our subjective interpretation of the passage of time, and of its influence on thinking and decision-making, plays an important part in the attitude of the strategic manager towards leadership and personal influence. We shall explore further, below, decision-making on the usage of time and, in Chapter 6, on the management of that usage.

Decisions on the usage of time

If the quality of time usage is targeted as a focus of organizational improvement, then this will eventually require new decisions at individual level – decisions, which have a very definite emotional content. Before these decisions can be made, the barriers to the growth of vision, set out in Chapter 3, need to be overcome. This will happen either by force of circumstance, or through a more organized, strategic intent.

To give a flavor of the adjustments that can then become possible, the story 'Why don't you whistle any more, Daddy?' is reproduced below. This story, created in the process of a corporate development project focused on effective time usage, reflects its author's personal experience and wish to contribute to others' thinking in this area.

'WHY DON'T YOU WHISTLE ANY MORE, DADDY?'

The general manager walked out of his client's reception area, crossed the car park and slid into the leather seat of his company car. He felt particularly satisfied with the way this meeting had gone and was especially pleased with his own contribution to the sealing of this afternoon's contract. His sales manager had even remarked how valuable his input had been during one of the more difficult parts of the discussion.

As he drove through the town, he looked at the clock. It was 3.30 pm. It was 1 hour and 20 minutes' drive back to head office, which meant he would get there just as others were leaving. Alternatively, it was just 20 minutes to his home. Normally he would have gone back to the office and worked for another two hours or so, clearing up paperwork while no one else was there, safe from interruption.

Today he was content with himself, proud of his contribution to the sales effort. He decided to return home early and surprise his wife and take the opportunity to welcome home the kids from school.

As he pulled into the driveway his young son, now 7 years old and just beginning to appreciate school, was walking down the road, satchel over his arm and talking with a couple of friends. The general manager got out of his car and started to whistle as he lifted his briefcase and newspaper off the passenger seat. His son spotted him, ran the remaining 50 yards up the driveway and jumped up at him, delighted to see he was home early for once.

'Are you going back to the office?' *'No, I've finished work for the day now. I'm going to be here for the rest of the evening.'* *'Oh great! I can show you what I can do on my new bike.'*

He put his son down and they walked together into the house. *'I heard you whistling; how come you don't whistle as much any more, Daddy? You always used to whistle. I remember hearing you whistling round the house when you were working or decorating, or doing jobs in the garden.'* *'Well, life is serious; sometimes I've got a lot on my mind. And to think and whistle is quite difficult, even for your Daddy.'*

He stopped in his tracks and thought about what he had just said, and realized that life these days in fact was always serious and there was always a great deal on his mind: new products, reorganization, acquisitions and so on - a whole list of things that required his personal involvement.

He took a beer from the fridge and walked out into the garden. It was a beautiful autumn evening and as he sat in the chair he started to think of what he had achieved over the last five years.

When they first moved into this house it was a wreck. At that time he spent many evenings and weekends redecorating and refurbishing the place to make it what it was now - a superbly kept example of late Victorian architecture. They had been careful to preserve all the interesting architectural details and had sympathetically extended the building over the garage to give more space. He remembered the long hours spent to make it that way. Well he had certainly created a good 'quality of life' for his family.

He was also satisfied with the way things were going at work but would not allow himself to think that progress still couldn't be made. He was constantly looking for new ways to improve the performance of the company. He had a competent team of people around him and again was proud of much of their work. He was delighted to be actively involved in some of the more detailed projects that were going on at the moment.

He pondered what his son had said and decided that the effort put in at work would eventually pay dividends for his home life. Just a few more years of these long hours, and then he'd be able to sit back and watch the team he'd built around him get on with the management of the company, while he would be needed for fewer hours and could devote them to longer-term planning, concentrating more on the possible directions in which to steer the company longer-term.

But by then, he suddenly realized, his son would be a teenager with his own circle of friends, out at weekends, and probably in the evenings. He would also be heavily involved in school work and sport. Perhaps at that age his son would not want his dad around too much. There and then, sitting in his garden that quiet autumn evening, he decided he was going to start spending more time with his family.

He walked inside the house, picked up his briefcase, brought it back out into the garden and looked at his diary. When was the next opportunity he could get home early on a Friday and spend a long weekend with his family? The following week was full: an important product launch and the annual exhibition. It would be impossible to get away. He would even have to spend two nights out, one of them being Friday. Saturday morning would be spent helping the troops to break down the exhibition and tying up the final loose ends, in terms of their marketing drive.

He looked forward a week and saw that it was the Hundred Percent Sales Club outing on the Friday, Saturday and Sunday. This he and his wife would have to attend. It was one of the things he insisted on doing. Being with the top performers in the sales team on a social weekend, just once a year, was not too much to ask.

He looked forward again to the end of October. It was now entering budget review time, getting ready for the new financial year in January. No, that would require some long hours and perhaps even for him to spend Saturday morning with the management accounts team.

He looked again and saw that in five weeks' time there would be an opportunity to take time off. He immediately entered, in pencil, 'Family Weekend'. Again, he looked down at what he was doing and realized he was writing in pencil with the anticipation that this could change, and if something urgent came up he was quite likely to subvert this family weekend in favour of sorting out whatever catastrophe or crisis was looming at that time.

Why was he doing this? The first time in a period of five weeks he could take his family away for a weekend---and here he was writing in pencil, in the full knowledge that he would probably break this engagement. He tried to rationalize and justify this. *'People need my input. I'm the general manager of the company. I have to lead by example and display my commitment to the people.'* This was a period of growth and the pressure was on everybody to put in as much as possible in order to achieve what it was they were seeking for themselves and their families.

He paused again. *'For themselves and their families.'* What was he saying?

In five weeks he couldn't afford one weekend with his family? *'Why am I bothering to work at this at all?'* Again, he justified this to himself. *'People want to see me there, see that I am putting in the long hours. They want to see me leading by example in terms of the amount of effort that is going into the new projects and the new products, the strategic implementation of the plans that have been carefully worked out over the past three or four years.'*

Well, of course, this was part of his responsibility. He accepted and held clear his leadership role, and one thing was for sure: he had led the organization through serious and long-lasting changes, and would continue to do so.

'Well,' he said to himself, *'if I can lead the people around me, if I can influence the marketplace, if we can grow 10 per cent exponentially over five years, then maybe I can also make changes and improvements in my own way of operating---including freeing up time for the family.*

'One condition: I have to make a commitment to this, in the same way that I make a commitment to pushing through the company's long-term projects.'

He looked at the principles under which he managed projects with his people. The first step was to act now, to make the decision and choose to do the things that he was going to plan. He picked up his diary again, scrubbed out the product launch and wrote in 'Family Weekend'. He looked further down the page and crossed out the entries for Wednesday in the following week. In it were a series of meetings being held by his staff. He had decided to attend them as an observer to get a feel for what was going on in those departments.

'No,' he said, *'this is not staying in my diary. I trust them. I know what's going on. They can report back. If they need me, they'll call me.'* He picked up the telephone and called his secretary, who was rather surprised to be instructed to cancel the three meetings he had on the Wednesday and to book it as a day's leave. She was even more surprised to be taking down, in shorthand, a memo to the marketing director and sales director concerning a product launch and to find herself noting in the desk diary that the general manager would not be available on the Friday and Saturday.

He wished her a pleasant weekend, put down the telephone and immediately started to map out a plan for guarding his time more rigorously. On one side of the page he put the necessary actions, on the other side he noted the impact this would have on the business.

'Guarding time - first step,' he wrote. When asked to commit time, he would evaluate this on the basis of (a) how important it was for him to be there, (b) who else could do this job in his place---and even benefit from the experience, and (c) what additional steps could be taken to enhance the outcome.

On the other side of the page he wrote, *'Maybe a surprise for other people. Will probably result, in the long term, in improved performance and motivation of those who are attending in my place.'*

Again he returned to the first side. *'Stop all token attendance of meetings.'* Impact on others: *'Probably a sigh of relief. They won't have to answer uninformed questions from the general manager. It may also provide those people with the security that the general manager is doing what the general manager ought to be doing and that they are being left to get on with their jobs, and therefore being more efficient.'*

He scanned back across to the other side of the page. He realized that not only was he freeing up his own time, in order to do the things that the general manager ought to be doing, but he was influencing developments in the culture of the company. In fact by continuing and extending these changes, he was likely to effect a medium- and long-term improvement in his senior management team and probably in many other employees of the company.

Having made his decision, he then discovered a further five items that could be attended to in this way, each opening up more time for effective involvement in his own specific areas of activity. He scanned his diary over the past month and noted, by the number of engagements he had fulfilled, that he had already been a very efficient user of time. Now he had found several creative steps enabling him to devote extra time to key activities, and achieve more as a consequence.

As he looked forward in his diary, he realized that he had just made the transition from being efficient to being efficient and *effective*. This satisfied him greatly as he looked forward to the coming weekend and the opportunity to enjoy some quality time with his family.

He whistled on his way back to the house, admiring the garden; and as he walked, he remembered that his son had wanted to show what he could do on his new bike. . . .

CHAPTER 6

Managing strategic relationships

Tactics: the strategic application of resources

For the Level 3 Leader, tactics are the application of resources towards objectives and aims. We may immediately think of resources as machinery or money, which provide topics for management decision-making. But the decision-making itself is a product of the application of the organization's or group's internal resources. Of these, the principal one is time, invested either in thinking or in meetings.

The resources, which form the focus of strategic decision-making are therefore time and people. And people spend their time thinking and communicating. It is the components of internal action which provide the fundamental resources for the growth of vision, and consequently for all strategy.

Research indicates that executives spend on average 22 per cent of their time in the activities we have called thinking, and 78 per cent in the activities we have bracketed under communicating.

Under pressure and in crisis, the 78 per cent grows, compensated for by less thinking time or much longer working hours.

Of the 78 per cent of time typically devoted to

communicating, some 65 per cent, on average, is spent 'listening', that is, not talking. Thus the application of the resource of time required for the growth of vision through strategic questioning, as defined in Chapter 3, is already in place! The time, however, is not used strategically.

Communication and the growth of vision

For the Level 3 Leader, communication is a tactic in the process of translation from vision and action.

The Indian elephant

The fundamental block to strategic communication is the same as the obstacle we have already identified in Chapter 3 as the most powerful barrier to the growth of vision; that is, we do not realize that internal and external actions are separate.

We are in the position of the blind men in the well-known story from India, in which they each come into contact with a different part of the elephant. The one who touches the tail thinks it's a rope, the one who touches the side of the elephant thinks it's the wall of a house, the one who comes into contact with a leg thinks it's a tree, and so on.

A similar problem can be encountered at board meetings! If eight people are grouped together to discuss a certain 'reality', not realizing they can only present the results of their own internal action, based on their personal vision (see Figure 6.1). Through an open exchange, it may be possible to reach a consensus which reflects a greater degree of objectivity than each is able to bring individually - a picture of the whole elephant, to which all contribute and on which all eventually agree.

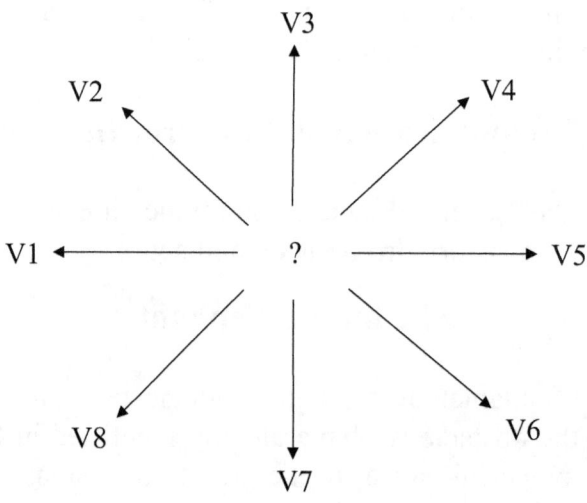

Figure 6.1 (The start of) a board meeting

For this to be possible meetings must be strategic, that is, for every meeting there must be a purpose, aims and one or more objective(s) towards which the meeting itself is a tactic.

When the agenda reflects these elements of strategy, it becomes possible for individual contributions to be strategic.

Vehicle for the growth of vision

The barriers to effective communication are identical to the barriers to the growth of vision (see Chapter 3). Strategic communication overcomes these barriers and consequently promotes the growth of vision.

For example, let us consider a discussion between two executives. If Executive A has viewpoint Y and Executive B has viewpoint Z, the manner in which the discussion unfolds will be influenced by the quality of vision, attitude and consequent internal action brought to it. Let us assume that neither executive has any concept of the possible gap between internal and external action. The executives consequently take their personal views to be the whole picture. This unseen attitude is typical of the closed level of management discussed in Chapter 2. What will happen?

Executive A expresses an opinion, which may trigger an opinion from Executive B - and the opinions are stated as if they are facts. Further opinions, memories and associations are triggered and stated back and forth. One executive may feel strongly about a certain aspect, and become more assertive. The other may happen to agree, or may resist.

The outcome of the discussion is haphazard, and quite possibly ineffectual. Listening, in this closed level, is mostly a matter of waiting for the next trigger. The lasting result may well be the reinforcement of each executive's initial prejudice, either about each other, or about the subject, or both.

Searching out the other's interpretation

In Level 2 of Leadership, the conduct of the discussion will be quite different. The executives will be aware that their own views are subjective, incomplete interpretations. Each will feel a need, in more or less equal proportions, to discover the other's interpretation; to enter, as it were, the realm of the other person's internal action. Each will also know, instinctively or as a result of study, the conversational devices to achieve this: open questions and attentive listening.

If the attitude of both participants is sufficiently attuned, an exchange of viewpoint may be possible. There will be a tendency on the part of each person to acknowledge, to validate, to accept the other's view as a component of the present situation, without immediate judgment. Executive A has contributed viewpoint Z; Executive B has contributed viewpoint Y. Now a productive conversation may be possible if a common purpose has been expressed in the agenda, and a common language has already been established between the participants.

Listening as the focal point of culture

The quality of listening ultimately dictates the quality of communication. If listening is attentive and active, it will raise new questions in the mind of the questioner. These may be questions about and for the other person, or they may be about the questioner's own vision, now brought into a different perspective.

One of the aspects of the transition from the second to the third Level of Leadership is the increasing tendency for listening

154

to result in questions in both participants' minds about the quality of the interaction between them.

If it is true, as research indicates, that communication occupies 78 per cent of executive time, and listening occupies 65 per cent of time spent in communication, then can we not say that the quality of culture depends [$(78\times65)/100 =$] 51 per cent on listening?

The quality of listening, parallel with that of management and leadership, ranges from closed to open to strategic. We need to study it!

The power of questions

Questions, like listening, occupy a central role in the language and communication of strategic decision-making. They can be part both of speaking and of listening. They define agenda. They define the order of strategic thinking and decision-making.

Questions have many specific powers. One is to focus attention and promote thought. By uncovering the true issues, they can provide information about perceptions. They can provide time for listening. Their influence can be almost magical for, insofar as they acknowledge the value of others' views and display interest in them, they can generate the possibility of cooperation. The more we find out about others, the easier it is to appreciate and understand them. Prejudice can be avoided, concurrence sought and empathy can develop.

Questions can also give information. The attentive listener can learn a great deal both from the questions and from the type of questions another is asking. A group of middle managers researching this question found results which interested them greatly: that people trust doctors who invest time in open questions; that barristers and analysts generate mistrust through their use of closed questions ('Do you think . . . ?', 'Isn't it the case that . . . ') to manipulate others.

The research also revealed the true champions of the open and even strategic question. They were not teachers, nor bosses, nor interviewers, nor authors, nor salespeople, nor professional practitioners, nor even researchers! They were kids! Kids really wish to find out, without manipulation!

What happens as we get older? Does our experience make us more, or less, receptive? What can be done to make sure that we are maintaining a distinction between vision and prejudice, and that we can see more than reflections of the past?

Archetypal business meetings

The transition from a closed to an open - and ultimately to a strategic – level of leadership culture includes the gradual up-grading of the quality of communication throughout an organization. This can begin with an ordering of the amorphous mass characteristic of closed communication into the ten archetypal meetings which underpin the conduct of open leadership. These are:

- The recruitment meeting
- The delegation meeting
- The appraisal meeting
- The reprimand meeting
- The dismissal meeting

- The team meeting
- The proposal meeting
- The brainstorming meeting
- The sales meeting
- The negotiation meeting.

In the remainder of this chapter we shall explore the nature of these meetings and their relation to the four strategic responsibilities. Ideally, this exploration is a practical one, through which our knowledge of communication, and therefore our vision, can grow.

For example, it is noticeable that, within seconds of meeting someone, we may have formed an opinion of that person. By what process is such an opinion formed? What happens between the moment we see a person and the moment at which we become aware of an attitude, reaction or feeling towards him or her?

A focus for personal research

This requires investigation! The visionary manager is continually aware of three underlying principles of human interaction, which again can be most interesting to analyse. The first is that we always influence others, and there is always a reaction. Once there is contact - even possibly when there isn't - there is some kind of impact.

Second, the entire outcome of an influence can be determined by a single detail. Any salesperson who has done everything necessary to secure an order, but loses the order through a careless remark, will know the truth of this.

Third, we can consciously influence the automatic reactions

of others. This truth of human suggestibility, which forms the underlying vision of all advertising, offers a rich vein of study which may also bring with it fundamental questions of responsibility.

The value of group research

All that has been said above on the subject of communication by individuals applies equally to communication within and between groups. Strategic communication by groups is the tactical part of a larger organizational strategy. For this role to be fulfilled, it must first be possible to generate constructive exchanges of interpretations within and between groups. This creates the possibility for meetings to become the vehicle for the growth of vision within and among groups.

As with individuals, such growth depends mainly on the ability of the group as a whole to study and to listen actively. In the context of groups, these aspects are reflected in the quality of agenda, in the quality of research and information flow between groups, and in the quality of internal discussion, which is itself dictated by the quality of personal influence of the group members.

A generic strategy for communication

As a guide for the research indicated above, Example 6.1 sets out a generic strategy for management communication.

The vision is a concise statement of the aspect of relatedness which will ideally inform all communication: that future results depend on the quality of vision at individual, group and organizational levels.

Based on this vision, the purpose of communication is seen

as a means to facilitate the growth of vision at these three levels! The strategic aims that will serve this purpose are the 'sideways' and 'downwards' strategic responsibilities.

Example 6.1
A generic strategy for communication

Vision

All future results depend on the quality of vision - personal, team and corporate.

Purpose

The purpose of communicating is to facilitate the growth of vision.

Strategic aims

1. Create and maintain the conditions in which direct reports can fulfill their potential.
2. Generate trust and cooperation with colleagues.
3. Enhance the organization's reputation.

Objectives

Specific to each manager's situation.

Tactics

Preparation and conduct of the ten archetypal business meetings.

The objectives - the measures of productivity in relation to aim - will necessarily be specific to each management situation. But important aspects of the tactics are universal, and it is to these that we shall now devote our attention.

Influencing downwards: environment creation

The influence downwards is the effect of one level of authority on the level immediately beneath it. While our focus here is on the business context, the principles given for this relationship can equally be applied in parent-child relationships, between central and regional government, in schools, in the relationship between an organization and its suppliers, or in any other relationship between a higher and a lower level of authority.

External and internal conditions

What are the conditions that make up the environment in which people can contribute fully? To this effect there are the external conditions of space (such as office space, machinery, distance from home, the physical working environment), time (working hours, holidays) and remuneration (salary package, car, bonuses, etc.).

There are also internal conditions, including the manner in which the contribution to be made is defined, articulated and reviewed. External and internal conditions are both a product of management culture.

The requirements for an effective influence downwards encompass both external and internal conditions. The external conditions of space, time and remuneration are recognized by Level 2 and Level 3 leaders as 'hygiene factors' - elements whose presence is unlikely to be motivating on their own, but whose absence or insufficiency is demotivating. It is important to ensure that they are correctly apportioned, and at the same time do not require frequent attention.

Once the external conditions are in place, the quality of the relationship is determined by the internal conditions. These are influenced mainly by the attitude and quality of thinking of the senior person through the conduct of six meetings specific to this relationship:

- The recruitment meeting
- The delegation meeting
- The appraisal meeting
- The reprimand meeting
- The dismissal meeting
- The team meeting

We shall investigate these meetings with the help of a series of templates which, taken together, form a third level of strategy.

Strategy within tactics

The planning of specific meetings marks the beginning of the third level of strategic awareness, which exists within the tactics of the strategic role definition. Each type of meeting can have a generic vision and purpose, which are derived from the generic strategic aims of communication (Example 6.1). Each meeting can also have its own strategic aims and objectives. The tactics of the meeting - a potential fourth level of awareness - will comprise internal and external actions during the course of the meeting.

The recruitment meeting

This is usually the first meeting between the employee and the organization. In many cases the recruitment process actually consists of a number of meetings, possibly conducted by a number of people. In considering the meeting, we shall bear in mind the larger process behind it.

We may also note that, while our focus is on the recruitment of a new employee, the principles apply equally in the appointment of temporary staff, consultants and suppliers of all kinds.

Generally speaking, the purpose of recruitment can be defined as to add a new tactical resource, where the important word is tactical. Recruitment, like everything else in strategic decision-making, is the product of strategic thinking. Checking the strategic value of proposed recruitment often reveals that there may be more effective ways of sourcing the extra help needed.

To serve this purpose, three strategic aims can be created as signposts for the direction of action: (1) to locate and attract the person or organization that will supply the contribution required; (2) to provide a smooth induction of the resource into the new role; and (3) to enhance the organization's reputation in the process.

From a generic point of view, we can establish an objective only at lowest common denominator level: that an appointment will be made by a certain date. The nature and application of this new resource needs to be clear for purposes of future decision-making.

In the case of an individual, this can be done through

creating a Role Definition, as illustrated in Chapter 5. The equivalent can also be adopted for a corporate supplier, to which all the comments made in Chapter 5 also apply. The recruitment meeting is part of tactics in the overall strategy.

When does this meeting between the organization and the prospective recruit begin? We have seen that once there is contact there is always an influence. Generally speaking, the contact does not begin with the first face-to-face interaction. By that time influences have already been exerted, perhaps through an advertisement, a telephone call, a letter or a screening interview with a recruitment consultant.

It may not have begun there. The potential recruit may already be familiar with the organization, or its reputation, through its products or services, through other employees, through familiarity with its buildings, through previous advertisements - in short, through the whole range of more or less subtle influences, which the organization, consciously or not, exerts within its wider environment.

While the face-to-face contact is the official starting point, this may take place years after the real beginning of the meeting between organization and recruit.

From the point of view of strategic decision-making, all the influences that can help shape a prospective recruit's image of the organization need to be planned. A good reputation in the labour market is as important as in any other market. For this reason, if recruitment consultants are used, care will be taken to manage the relationship with them according to the principles of leadership set out in this chapter. Particular care will be given to the handling of the relationship with unsuccessful candidates. They may have as strong an impact on the organization's reputation as those who are recruited!

In the same way, an advertisement for a position can be an advertisement for the organization as a whole. In an advertisement, the clarity of thought and expression is visible. How clearly is the vision communicated - the vision with which the recruitment process began? How has this been adjusted to appeal to the mentality of the target element of the labor market?

Assuming that the impersonal prelude to a face-to-face meeting produces a pool of talent from which the eventual recruit can be chosen, a great deal will now depend on the quality of personal interaction. The aim is to locate and attract the person who will - not who can or who might - provide the contribution required.

Failure in this can be very expensive. A person may be recruited who spends three months adjusting into the role, three months performing effectively, three months feeling increasingly disen-chanted and three months performing with minimal effect while seeking another post. A year has been spent, and paid for, which produced three months of fully effective work. Now the process will have to begin again, possibly with similar inefficiency. What can be done to ensure recruitment of the person who will perform?

Insofar as the closed and open levels of leadership thinking address this question, they respond with a range of approaches. The 'old-boy' network is the safe haven of closed management. When it is necessary to step beyond this, and make judgments about unknown characters, the main support is the CV (curriculum vitae). The Latin name corresponds suitably to the past-orientation of this dubious piece of paper. The CV can never give a complete picture of the person's career history, and even less of the subtle influences of other people on its contents. Even if it could be complete and objective, this gives no guarantee of future performance.

In the grey area between closed and open, techniques are used to try to indicate the prospective recruit's character and potential. These include various forms of tests, often with a multiple choice question format, but they will always suffer from the limitations of any system that tries to pigeon-hole human ability and performance.

Research indicates that managers only trust such approaches to the extent that they correspond to their pre-formed opinion of the prospective recruit. If this opinion is confirmed, it is a good test; if not, it is regarded as dubious. Although this means that personality and other tests may find greater currency in situations such as recruitment, if there is no history in the relationship, they still cannot indicate how a person will perform.

It is much more relevant to discover the potential recruit's vision. A sensitive interviewer can gain more information by this method than by any other standard technique. Indeed, there is no foolproof technique - it all depends on the vision and attitude of the interviewer. If this attitude is right, security for the future can be built. The candidate's ideas and interpretation of his or her own past career, development potential and existing knowledge of the organization will display to the sensitive interviewer the candidate's level of responsibility. Ultimately it is this, combined with the quality of leadership from above and the required basic ability for the role, that will determine the quality and permanence of future performance.

Somewhere in Level 2 of Leadership lies another grey area in which interviews are conducted according to a system of questioning. These are developed from questions that have given a degree of success in the past. On paper, they may seem to be the type of questions a strategic manager would ask, but they have been reduced to stereotypes, which will usually be sensed by the interviewee and which reflect an inability of the interviewer to be spontaneous, either in asking questions or in receiving responses.

This type of interviewer may also be less than inadequate in 'selling' the organization - that is, in relating the characteristics of the internal and external action of the organization to those of the candidate.

Through the recruitment meeting, the vision of the organization and the vision of the prospective recruit must be exposed and juxtaposed. The interviewer must be responsible for this. The vision of the organization, in this case, is not the vision featured in the annual report or marketing literature: it is the vision that has led directly to the recruitment currently taking place.

If this exposition of two visions is done with care and insight, then there will be at least two productive consequences: first, the most fitting recruit will be selected and, second, those not suitable may have the possibility of remaining enthusiastic about the organization.

The Level 3 Leader, aware of the vital significance of the recruitment process, will take a strategic interest in the detail of this interaction between the organization and the outside world.

Creative ways may be found for assessing the attitude and responsiveness of candidates. These may include exposure of short-listed applicants to likely future colleagues, in a planned way. Those skilled in the management of group dynamics may also devise ways to group applicants together in a manner that will help reveal the more subtle aspects of character and ability to contribute as needed.

The quality of recruitment may be regarded as the biggest single influence on the quality of time management throughout the organization, and the level 3 leader will treat it with a corresponding level of importance. From the process itself will emerge a strategy for the first months of the new recruit's role, encapsulated in the Role Definition.

The recruitment process aims to find the person or resource who will make the contribution that is required. The process itself cannot do more than establish the potential and the starting point. The remainder will depend on the quality of subsequent leadership.

The delegation meeting

In strategic leadership, authority needs to be increased gradually, and responsibility should have the chance to grow.

Delegation is the transfer of authority; it is a further medium for the growth of vision, through which responsibility can be nourished. To the lower level of authority, it offers the possibility of new experience, new decision-making and greater influence; to the higher level of authority, it offers a way of rewarding responsibility displayed at a lower level, of building expertise within the organization and, above all, of creating uncommitted time at senior level.

While the external action of delegation exists in all three levels of leadership, the character of its internal action, and therefore its quality, again varies greatly between the levels.

The closed manager, and to some extent the open manager, will delegate for his or her own interest, rather than the interest of the delegatee or of the organization, to which they may be relatively blind. The closed manager will seek to delegate responsibility rather than authority. This back-to-front approach to delegation is the essence of the worst forms of manipulation of human beings, carrying with it all kinds of emotional blackmail and subtle threat.

The fashionable term empowerment indicates a shift intended to reverse this wrong relationship between responsibility and authority.

In delegating, the closed leader will give orders at tactical level. The delegatee is required to perform accurately, but not to think or plan. The open leader differentiates between objective and route, inviting the delegatee's input into the route. The strategic leader carries this differentiation further, planning the devolution of decision-making as part of the evolution of the organization, linked to the personal development of its members.

In principle, the strategic leader will communicate the key aspects of the strategy in question, which have already been decided. Depending on the delegatee's expertise and potential, this may be the whole strategy including tactics, or it may only be vision and purpose, with aims to be agreed together and the planning of objectives and tactics to be left to the delegatee. In this way, delegation becomes an education in strategic thinking.

The appraisal meeting

The appraisal meeting provides the interface between two separate yet integral parts of strategic decision-making: the strategy of the organization and the strategy of the individual. The purpose of this meeting is to align the appraisee's personal and career development with corporate strategy.

The strategic leader will therefore use the appraisal meeting (1) to create harmony between his or her own vision and that of the appraisee, (2) to renew the basis of cooperation and (3) to create opportunities for growth. This will produce a development plan, which may then be reflected in an updated role definition.

The level 3 leader knows that, if this development plan is to be practicable, the appraisee must be motivated towards it. Therefore, the more the plan can reflect the appraisee's own aspirations, the better. These must provide the starting point of all discussion, and must be prepared in advance by the appraisee. Insofar as the past is discussed, the relevant areas are the successes achieved and lessons learned, which can point the way to the future through the confidence they generate and the example they set.

To the perception of positive developments that have already happened can be added the perception of current potential - latent capability yet to be made visible. The appraisee's perception of these, together with current ideas for what is needed in terms of development, must form the basis of the discussion. The appraisor will listen and add suggestions. Working together, a plan can be created, which includes elements of both visions and yet constitutes something new that could only have been created as a result of the meeting.

For the level 2 leader, the appraisal process may be quite different. The meeting is seen as something between a judgment of the past and a medium for numerical objective-setting. Neither party looks forward to it - especially if some kind of grading of performance, related to salary increase or bonus, is involved.

The danger in this approach is that the aspirations of the appraisee are not articulated and cannot be connected to corporate strategy - if there is one! The senior participant occupies the more or less uncomfortable position of judge, and the conversation focuses mostly on the past - perhaps on `remedying' it. The usefulness of the meeting can be reduced further by a focus on form-filling, signatures and other products of well-intentioned but fundamentally misguided ideas about how to generate improvement.

In level 1 leadership, this meeting either does not exist or has no impact on individual, group or corporate performance. There may only be a salary review.

The reprimand meeting

The level 3 leader feels strongly the responsibility to create and maintain an environment in which potential will be fulfilled.

From time to time this will include a need to correct and realign the performance of a direct report. In strategic decision-making, the purpose of a meeting in which such realignment will be generated is very clear: to provide help.

In general, there are three aims that provide the focus in giving such help. First, the leader needs to be clear about the relationship between his or her own conduct and the perceived need for realignment. This may reveal a different source of the problem.

Second, both in private and during the meeting with the direct report, the leader needs to establish, or re-establish, the principle(s), previous agreement(s), rule(s), policy or policies at stake.

Third, there is a need to secure steps for concrete indication that the realigned basis of action is reflected in performance.

The objective of a reprimand meeting will therefore be a concrete plan for realigned action. Tactics towards this will include thorough preparation of the facts and of the principle that has been flouted. During the meeting, the principle and the facts will be contrasted. In level 3 leadership, there is no personal confrontation: only a careful juxtaposition of principle and fact, made in a positive framework which allows and encourages the direct report to influence the way forward.

In leadership levels 2 and 1 this meeting will be a more emotional affair. The level 2 leader is likely to tell the direct report what is wrong, and what to do about it; the level 1 leader may use the meeting only to off-load his or her own negativity. This is unlikely to be productive.

To be helpful, and to create the possibility of new understanding, the leader has to be unemotional in the communication. This may come not so much from superhuman self-control, but rather from seeing the situation differently and more completely - an indication of a need for help.

In the event of a repeated need, the level 3 leader will ensure that the concrete agreements that emerge are translated into the role definition.

The dismissal meeting

It almost inevitably happens in the course of the life of organizations that, the vision of a leader and a direct report will be irreconcilably opposed. Depending on which is the more dissatisfied party, this will result in either a resignation or a dismissal.

The level 3 leader understands that, in general, the need for a dismissal means that some kind of management mistake has been made previously. This may have been in recruitment or in the management of the direct report's performance. Based on this, the purpose of the meeting will be to secure a smooth, harmonious transition.

In level 3 leadership, there are typically three aims which form part of a generic strategy for dismissal. The first is to secure the active collaboration of the employee. The second is to handle the matter in such a way that the employee can still become a 'walking advertisement' for the organization, following the dismissal. The third is that, through the process of dismissal, the messages that subsequently ripple through the organization will have a whole-some effect on the culture.

To agree and secure a concrete plan that meets these aims, the tactics will most likely include a short meeting in which the organization's decision is communicated, supported by irrefutable evidence of inadequate performance and balanced with a concrete plan for a smooth transition.

In leadership levels 1 and 2, the conduct and resolution of these meetings will be relatively haphazard, since they will depend so much on aspects of vision, attitude and internal action that have received inadequate attention until this point.

The team meeting

Team meetings, whether at board, senior, middle or junior executive level, are expensive! If they are used to promote and monitor individual performance by the team members, then, from the point of view of the third level of leadership, such expense will not be justified, for each member will spend long periods of time listening to issues that he or she cannot influence directly.

The level 3 leader organizes and conducts team meetings based on a need to nurture the understanding of strategic responsibility. Their purpose is to promote trust, confidence and cooperation among the team. When this is secured, the same qualities are more likely to exist between the direct reports of the team members.

To achieve such trust, confidence and cooperation, the visionary leader will generally have three aims in mind: first, to create awareness among the team of each member's strategies and of current or potential overlaps; second, to develop strategies for issues which transcend the specific areas of authority of each individual; and, third, to coordinate the team's cultural influence within and outside the organization.

The objective of team meetings will be a plan for which each member is committed to carrying out at least one concrete action. If this is not the outcome, then the leader will need to review the agenda and conduct of the meeting, and reassess whose attendance is necessary and valuable.

Level 3 leaders regard team meetings as too expensive to be used for the dissemination of information. This is done in advance, so that questions and proposals can be prepared and concisely presented during the meeting.

Influencing upwards

The influence upwards is the influence of one level of authority on the level immediately above it. The principles for this relationship apply wherever it exists in organizational and private life. In level 3 leadership, the vision on which conduct of this influence is based is that current and future authority will depend on the quality of contribution made.

A child may earn an increase in authority through making a contribution to housework or gardening. This may take the form of pocket-money, or of having decision-making power over a section of the garden. In the same way, a member of an organization can expect a relationship to exist between the authority given and the responsibility which then characterizes its exercise.

This simple relationship tends to be obscured by two common factors in organizations. The first is that most managers confuse the time spent on relationships with their importance. Much more time tends to be spent with direct reports than with the boss. This is probably inevitable, and certainly desirable. Yet which relationship is the more important? It has to be the relationship upwards, because the existence of that relationship is the source of authority for the relationship downwards. This fact is overlooked by many managers who already have a good relationship upwards. The consequence may be that they fail to plan and manage this relationship as carefully as they might.

The second factor which tends to obscure the essence of the relationship upwards is that the senior manager fails to focus on and fulfill the relationship downwards. The junior executive's environment is not consciously created to enable that person to fulfill his or her potential. This means that the senior person may not be promoting the development of the junior person. In many cases, in open and especially closed management, the higher authority blocks the development of the lower, whether deliberately or not.

The strategic responsibilities inherent in strategic decision-making require reciprocal and simultaneous growth. The senior person cannot fulfill his or her responsibility downwards without the junior fulfilling his or her responsibility upwards, and vice versa.

In general, there are three strategic aims that form useful signposts for action in order to make a full contribution. The first is to be aware of the superior's aims and objectives. This means that these have first to be formulated and communicated by the superior! The second aim is to provide solutions. The third is to generate quality time for the senior person.

The concrete proof that these aims are in place will be the existence of a stimulating role definition, demonstrating their presence in the specific circumstances. The tactics will be the usage of all time that is dedicated to the organization. In strategic decision-making, all time usage is visibly connected to the contribution upwards. The element of time usage specific to the relationship upwards is the proposal meeting.

The proposal meeting

The proposal meeting is based on a vision of one or more aspects of contribution - either the junior person's, or the senior person's, or both.

We can identify three generic strategic aims for the conduct of the meeting: to relate the message to the senior person's attention span, to focus on the benefit for the senior - in relation to his or her own strategy - and to make it easy for him or her to say `Yes!'

The objective of the meeting is agreement from the senior person on at least one concrete step to be taken, which requires his or her assent. Tactics towards this will include careful preparation of the benefits to the decision-maker of the proposed change and the precise step for which agreement is sought.

Influencing 'sideways'

The influence sideways is the effect that a person or group has on other people or groups at an equivalent level of authority. This influence is exerted within the organization, among colleagues and peers, and externally. From the point of view of level 3 leadership, the quality of internal meetings determines the quality of corporate culture, and the quality of external meetings determines the quality of the organization's influence.

Based on this vision of influence, the generic sense of purpose that underpins any strategy for these relationships corresponds to the strategic responsibilities we have already defined. For the internal lateral influence, this is to generate trust and cooperation.

For the external lateral influence, it is to enhance the reputation of the organization.

Once again, we can identify generic strategic aims which provide signposts for action towards the fulfillment of purpose. For the influence on colleagues and peers, the first aim is to be fully aware of their strategies and interests. As long as this aim is served, it is possible to work towards the two further aims: to find opportunities to nurture common interests, and to develop synergy between direct reports - one's own and the colleague's.

The objectives - the concrete measures of productivity towards these aims - will be reflected in a plan for collaboration with each colleague. Elements of this plan are likely to impact on, and be influenced by, a joint influence upwards.

Aims for external influence will normally include customers and suppliers, but there are many other external contacts who are outside these categories. One such group, as we have seen, are unsuccessful candidates for recruitment. Prospective investors, the family and social contacts of employees, former employees, city analysts, organizations with potential for a future merger or takeover, and many more existing or potential contacts, can be on the receiving end of individual, group and corporate influence.

The first aim towards enhancing the reputation of the organization is to be clear about the purpose of the contact. The second is to be clear about the strategic responsibility that is being served.

What appears to be, or feels like, an equal level of authority on a personal level may actually represent an influence upwards or downwards between groups or organizations. The third aim is to link the contact's interests with those of the organization. As with internal influence, the generic objective will be the production and maintenance of a plan for collaboration.

There are three types of meeting that provide the main vehicles for the lateral influence, both internal and external. They are the brainstorm meeting, the sales meeting and the negotiation meeting.

The brainstorm meeting

The vision on which the brainstorm meeting is based is that new ideas can be generated through a process of thought association.

As one thought triggers another, the familiar ideas are cleared out of the way to make room for the less familiar, more original possibilities.

The purpose of a brainstorm meeting is to foster the growth of vision. There are three aims towards this. The first, and perhaps the most difficult, is the creation of a non-judgmental environment. Any hint that ideas are being judged as they are spoken will hinder and limit the possibilities of thought association. The second aim is to prepare creative questions. The quality of these will influence very strongly the quality of thought, and therefore the subsequent decision. The third aim is that everyone present should contribute ideas.

The objective of a brainstorm is normally the production of database of ideas for subsequent analysis and decision. This second element, calling for a different type of thinking, can be carried out at a different time and place, even by different people - perhaps those who have responsibility for the outcome of the eventual decision.

Tactics to secure this objective will include finding a neutral venue (ideally away from the workplace), including non-specialists in the meeting, recording all the ideas and, for the leader only, preparing questions that will assist the process.

The sales meeting

The term sales meeting applies equally whether the item being sold' is a product, a service or an idea. This meeting is based on the assumption that others may benefit from help in either the formulation or the implementation of their strategy - or both. The purpose is always to assist the other person to translate his or her own vision into action.

That person's vision may not be clear, so the first aim is to help clarify the other person's vision, purpose and aims in relation to the service, product or idea under discussion. A second aim will be to help him or her to make the leap from aims to objectives - to establish what will be a concrete measure, desirable in the context of an aim. The third aim will be to facilitate a decision for tactics towards this.

The objective will be the generation of new action. This may take the form of a simple exchange of resources, such as buying a pair of shoes at a certain price, or a plan for collaboration over a period of time. The tactics towards this will include well-prepared questions to help articulate vision and the acknowledgement and extension of constructive lines of thought.

Since decisions for change can be emotional, the salesperson needs to provide help against the influence of fear. There is also a time to stop talking: silence may allow a clear perspective on what is really needed, and thus assist a productive decision.

Exhortation and clever manipulation are not part of the sales process in Level 3 leadership. If the reputation of the organization is to be enhanced, and if trust and cooperation are to be built internally, then the only satisfactory sale is one that provides a constructive element of the buyer's strategy.

The negotiation meeting

In the negotiation meeting there is already agreement to agree. This is the vision on which the meeting is based. Its purpose is to formulate the details. For this there will be three aims: to exchange vision, purpose and aims in connection with the matter in question; to find the common ground; and to translate this into concrete steps. The objective will be, once again, a plan for collaboration. Tactics will include the prior preparation of the communication of vision, purpose and aims, and the identification of parameters for the contribution required and the contribution offered.

Written communication

The visionary leader is interested in written communication for two main reasons; one is to provide sources of information and ideas for strategic decision-making; the other is to safeguard strategic decisions that have been made.

Compared to closed and open managers, the visionary manager uses written communication relatively little. In the lower levels, more written communication is needed to shore up relationships, but once the relationships are stronger and are underpinned by the sense of strategic responsibility, much less is required.

Part of the research, which all executives may find productive, is to examine very carefully the real reasons for their use of written communication. Why is it necessary, and does it actually provide what is needed in its current form?

Such research can itself generate ideas and information for strategic decision-making, resulting in new action.

CHAPTER 7

Moving between Levels

Organizational growth through the levels of leadership

We have identified and explored the nature of three distinct levels of leadership. Labelling them generically *closed, open* and *strategic*, we have also given them specific titles for individual, team and organizational contexts (see Figure 7.1).

Dimension	*Manager/ leader*	*Team*	*Organization*
3rd (Strategic)	Visionary	Organic	Service-oriented
2nd (Open)	Active	Dynamic	Goal-oriented
1st (Closed)	Passive	Static	Past-oriented

Figure 7.1 Three levels in three contexts

The articulation of these three levels in each context provides a framework in which the *integration* of personal, team and organizational development becomes possible, meaningful and desirable.

In Parts 1 and 2 of this book we have examined ideas and ways of thinking characteristic of the first, second and, especially, third Levels of leadership. The question naturally arises: What has to be done? What is necessary in order to build a service-oriented organization - a business that is itself strategic, in which managers have visionary leadership qualities and in which teams operate and grow organically?

Today's conditions call increasingly for a capability within organizations of all types to speed up the translation of vision into action. This translation is our definition of strategy. The demand to be part of it and to contribute to it extends increasingly throughout the organization.

Building the strategic organization

Chief executives are increasingly aware of the need to build a strategic, service-oriented organization in which strategic thinking - as set out in Part 2 of this book - can become a central feature of corporate culture.

What must we do to build such a culture? How can we overcome the barriers to the growth of vision set out in Chapter 3? How can we generate an active interest throughout the organization in the quality of decision-making, time usage and personal influence? How can we translate this interest into strategic role definitions that are integrated and acted upon across the organization?

How, in short, can a whole organization make the transition from a closed, through an open, to a strategic culture?

The process: creating new management agenda

In essence, the process for moving between levels can be seen as a process of transition to new management agenda. Undertaken by the organization as a whole, it represents the research, based on individual strategic questioning, already discussed in Chapter 1 (see Figure 7.2). Its nature will be outlined in this chapter.

There often comes a point when the chief executive sees that the most important issue on his or her own agenda is to find a way of moving the organization as a whole from past- or goal-orientation to service-orientation. The key strategic decision is the decision to create a strategic organization. As soon as this is seen, doubts may be raised about the capacity of current executives to be part of the organization's future.

There is no universal answer: each organization has its own set of circumstances and its own people. Yet experience reveals three important points. First, the chief executive's expectations can often be exceeded in this area. It may even be that one of the first changes to take place is a change in the way the chief executive views the members of the board or senior management team.

Second, those who cannot make the jump tend to recognize this during the process, and it may help them to make another kind of change.

Third, the well-known Peter Principle - that 'managers are promoted to their position of incompetence' - underlines the truth that most managers are in a role for which they do not feel fully prepared.

Leadership Development

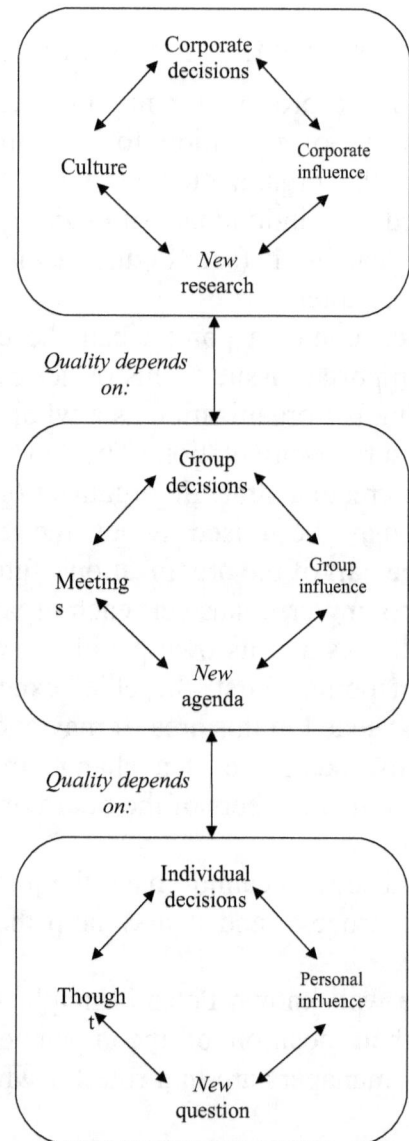

Figure 7.2 New management agenda linked to individual questioning and research.

For many executives, the process of strategic development outlined in this chapter compensates for this lack and helps them to fulfill a potential they always suspected they had but could never articulate.

Ultimate responsibility - and the bottom-up, top-down question

The chief executive is ultimately responsible for the quality of corporate culture, as well as for structure and strategy. This is strongly borne out by the case studies detailed in this chapter.

At the same time, it is true that it is difficult, if not impossible, for the chief executive to exert a direct influence at middle and junior management levels. This difficulty - reinforced, perhaps, by the unwillingness or incapacity of some chief executives to respond to this aspect of their role - has led to the spreading of the notion of 'bottom-up' culture change.

In the closed and, to some extent, the open levels of leadership, many aspects of corporate life are relatively haphazard, and there may be minor cultural shifts, which occur independently of senior management influence. But to become a strategic, service-oriented organization requires a growth of vision at all levels. This will certainly mean that the style of influencing both downwards and upwards must develop. This means *evolution*, not *revolution*.

It can only be demoralizing for intelligent executives at any level to be exposed to a higher quality of thinking and communicating that they cannot recognize in the conduct of their seniors. And the value of such exposure, and any growth of vision that results, may be quickly eliminated by the ingrained habits of the senior management style.

The building of the strategic organization must be championed, whether overtly or not, by the chief executive and senior management team - beginning with the decision to initiate the organization's movement between levels.

The most strategic decision

It is difficult to think of a decision that can serve the four strategic responsibilities (see Chapter 2) more fully than the decision to develop a strategic culture. This single decision can have an improving influence on all future decision-making within and on behalf of the organization.

It may also be the most difficult decision to make. The very nature of a strategic development process means that the future benefits may be impossible to assess concretely, while the investment of time and money are only too clear! And there is never an ideal time - there are always holiday periods, mini-crises, restructuring, the impending arrival of a new director or human resources manager, etc.

All this assumes that the question has been raised in the first place. This will never happen in many organizations, or in others it may not happen until it is too late, on account of the *barriers to the growth of vision* outlined in Chapter 3.

Four principles for the growth of corporate vision

If corporate vision is to grow, this means that the vision of individuals and groups must also grow. In all cases, the first step is to articulate current vision.

We have seen that vision exists in some form in all three levels of leadership. In the first level (closed leadership) it may take the form of unarticulated assumptions that have accumulated over an extended period. In the second level (open leadership), vision may take the form of stated objectives or ideals, most likely with hidden assumptions in the background.

The creation of a picture of current vision across a management group - a *vision audit* - is itself a project requiring considerable expertise in facilitation. Once this is completed, and individual and group vision have been to some extent articulated, it is possible for growth to begin.

Our case histories will illustrate that, providing certain principles are observed, it is generally most effective for managers to work together in groups of eight or nine individuals of broadly equivalent levels of authority.('Vertical' groups - made up of managers at different levels of authority - may also work well, usually at a later stage.)

The four key principles concern fundamental aspects of the growth of vision and its consequent effect on performance. Since, generally, management and related education do not observe these principles, we shall explore them in some detail.

First principle: work on strengths

In some human resource departments, it has become fashionable to talk of 'competencies'. These are lists of desirable attributes and abilities for managers. The competencies for a particular job are listed, the manager's boss decides where the manager has inadequacies in terms of the list of competencies, and the manager is sent on training courses to remedy the inadequacies.

This is an approach to education and training related to the first or second rather than the third level of leadership. The dangers in it may indicate why many chief executives are justifiably sceptical of traditional business school and related approaches. As one chief executive said: 'I want brilliant people, not just competent people!' The main danger is that it will not affect performance because, as every sportsperson or musician knows, you improve by working, first, on your strengths. By acknowledging and fostering strengths, you help your all-round performance to be raised and give yourself the confidence and motivation needed to work on weaker areas.

To focus only on areas for improvement risks stagnation in the strong areas and the loss of the energy for improvement, which is related to the level of confidence.

A second flaw is the concept that executives will necessarily decide on an improvement just because someone else considers it to be a good idea! We are all most interested in our own ideas, which means that our own vision, when stimulated and given an environment for growth, is the most likely source of lasting improvements.

A further mistake can be generated by the idea that separate elements of management and leadership can be improved quite independently of each other. We have seen that the qualities of, for example, thinking, decision-making, time management and communication have a close interrelationship and cannot be separated from leadership. A lack of knowledge of this relationship indicates a lower degree of vision.

Perhaps the greatest value of competencies, as we shall see below, is their use in the expansion of vision, by encouraging groups of executives to design their own competencies!

Second principle: imitate the natural learning process

Life provides us with a natural learning process, which we have already studied in Chapter 3 (see Figure 7.3).

This natural learning process features a series of situations in which there is disharmony between vision and action. When we respond with the combination of question, internal action, decision and external action illustrated in Figure 7.4, we are learning!

The important point from the view of management and leadership education is that learning involves a series of situations, each including external action. This means experience. The classroom, lecture or reading/video-watching/tape-listening experience may expand vision, but this expansion will only be temporary, and is soon diminished by a return to habitual work patterns.

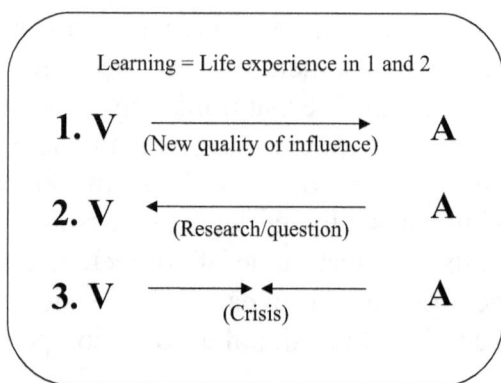

Figure 7.3 The value of disharmony between vision and action.

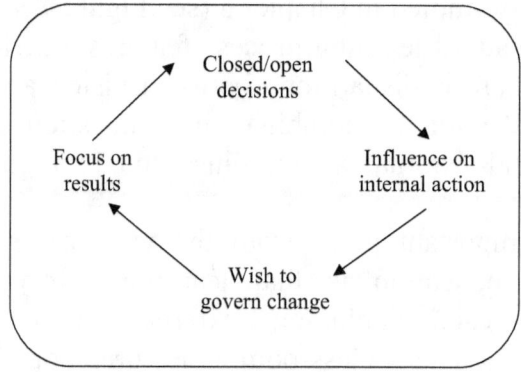

Figure 7.4 Open (learning) leadership culture (see Chapter 2).

Leadership development programmes based on various types of outdoor activity and adventure recognize the need for practical and shared experience but may fail to translate the key messages into the life of the organization.

The strategic development process must include opportunities for vision to expand, for new decisions to result which can then be put into practice, and for feedback to be generated which will give rise to a new breed of question, feeding further expansion of vision, and so on.

There is consequently a need for an input of questions that will raise awareness of where disharmony exists, actually or potentially, between vision and action. This must be done in the context of a process, which also provides opportunities for the adaptation of vision and the implementation of new decisions.

Since these questions, by definition, do not yet exist productively within the organization, they must be introduced from outside the current culture.

Third principle: a unique development path for each executive

Pulling the first two principles together, we can see that effective development will include the opportunity for each individual to become aware of his or her own relative strengths and weaknesses, and to decide on how to develop both of these areas, in the context of an overall set of attributes and abilities agreed on by the group.

This means that each executive will design his or her own unique personal development path, in the context of the general direction of the group's development. The guidance needed is a subtle blend of example and facilitation.

The possibility thus exists for an accelerated version of the natural learning process. To lead such a process is a delicate and demanding role. For full effectiveness, a fourth principle also applies.

Fourth principle: use the live issues

Resistance to the idea of management education is often, perhaps rightly, based on the theoretical nature of lectures and classroom approaches. If expanded vision is to result in new qualities of decision-making and influence, there must be a connection to the live issues.

A fourth principle of strategic development is that each individual manager's current issues should form the medium for experimentation and provide the material for study. This again places stringent demands on the quality of facilitation of the development process.

A selection of case histories

The development process indicated was pioneered by small-to medium-sized organizations in the late 1980s.We shall study how a selection of these companies responded to the possibilities inherent in developing a strategic culture between 1988 and 1994.

During 1988 and 1989, over 1000 chief executives in the UK were invited by Mitchell Leadership Consulting to explore ideas for strategic cultural development based on the four principles outlined above. Their companies spanned the full range of industry and commerce, and public sector organizations such as police forces also participated.

Some 120 of these chief executives, started to work with

Mitchell Leadership Consulting , and approximately half of them participated in a series of experimental Chief Executive Development Programmes promoted and led by Mitchell Leadership Consulting at the Institute of Directors and other venues in London and the UK between 1988 and 1991.

Approximately 50 of the chief executives who participated in these first programmes subsequently decided to invest in further work by Mitchell Leadership Consulting, geared to the development of the senior, middle and junior management strata. Through this work, the ideas and practices set out in Parts 1 and 2 of this book were pioneered, tested and brought to a fully developed form.

Similar needs: different starting points

To illustrate important aspects of the movement of an organization between levels of management, we shall follow the development of four companies who worked with Mitchell Leadership Consulting during the period 1988 to 1994.They are: Microsoft, Life Sciences International plc, Glynwed Metal Services and STA Travel.

These organizations operate in contrasting industries, and had development requirements in the late 1980s, which, at first sight, appeared quite different. Under closer scrutiny, it became clear that it was only the starting points that were different; the underlying need was common to all four.

Management skills for former technical and sales specialists Microsoft is one of the world's leading suppliers of software for personal computers, its products including the top-selling MS-DOS and Windows. Microsoft in the UK is a sales and technical support operation. In the late 1980s rapid growth was anticipated for the coming years, and Microsoft had perceived a clear strategic development need.

This development need had two key elements: first, to instill a high level of management and leadership ability among young, relatively inexperienced managers who had emerged from sales and technical backgrounds; second, to build a strong foundation of corporate management practices and attitudes as a basis for future growth.

Profitability, customer awareness and continuous improvement

Shandon Scientific is the largest subsidiary of Life Sciences International plc and the leading European manufacturer of cytology and histology equipment and consumables for clinical laboratories. In 1989 it had 230 employees and a turnover of £10 million.

In 1988, a new managing director was appointed. Increased competition was on the horizon from Japan and the USA, and the new director saw a clear need to improve profitability and productivity, to build company-wide customer awareness and to lay the foundation for the development of an ethic of continuous improvement throughout the organization. This would include the strengthening of daily management practice on the part of experienced managers, and the creation of greater responsiveness through devolving authority for decision-making.

A strategic need for a more flexible culture

Glynwed Metal Services is a division of Glynwed International plc, employing approximately 1000 people and distributing and processing aluminium and aluminium products, metal alloys and stainless steel.

The companies within the division, with brand names such as Aalco and Amari, had been built up over a period of two and a half decades to form the largest independent metals distribution business in the UK. By 1989, when they came under the ownership of Glynwed, the total number of locations in the UK, Canada, USA and Europe exceeded 50.

The takeover by Glynwed came at the end of a decade of rapid growth, much of it through acquisitions. While much of the historical success could be attributed to the autonomy of each geographical unit, individual managers were entrepreneurial, sales oriented and very independently minded. The company had grown too big for a fragmented approach to the marketplace, and increasingly found that branches were in competition with each other for the same business.

In 1988 it was decided that a catalyst was needed to create the atmosphere for change and a flexible, more mature culture.

The approach used by Glynwed Metal to create a service-oriented culture was based on three initial requirements.

First, to enable long-serving and proved regional, branch and sales managers to re-evaluate their style of people-management and communication. This was seen as essential in order to maintain and enhance competitiveness in an increasingly tight market.

Second, there was a strategic need to facilitate the

assimilation of the business as a whole into Glynwed International, which required a minimum return on assets and year-on-year profit growth. Third, in the light of new competition - especially from Europe - and a changing market, to prepare senior management for strategic challenges ahead. As it turned out, these were to include major cost-cutting programmes during and beyond the recession, the sale of the US business, the merging of several UK branches and, eventually, further acquisitions.

Strategic capability and professionalism

The fourth company, STA Travel, operates throughout the UK, Europe, USA and Asia Pacific to serve the travel needs of young independent travellers. Worldwide turnover in the year to March 1995 was US$375 million. In all its markets, STA Travel operates through a comprehensive network of retail shops and agents.

There were three perceived needs, which led to STA Travel's strategic partnership with Mitchell Leadership Consulting, which began in the UK in 1989. First, there was a need to broaden the management base. The UK managing director foresaw a period of expansion, and was convinced that senior and middle management needed to become involved in both the formulation and the secure implementation of long- and medium-term strategy.

Second, there was a need to raise the level of professionalism throughout the organization, as competition grew stronger. This would also contribute to STA Travel's ability to develop long-term relationships with their major suppliers, the airlines. The third need was that of developing high-quality customer relations management.

Dissatisfaction with conventional options

Faced with this variety of strategic needs, each of these four organizations had investigated and even experimented with a number of training and consultancy options. These included business schools, conventional business training organizations and accountancy-based consultancies.

Their experience with such organizations had, in general, been less than satisfactory from the point of view of corporate strategy.

Training courses may have been interesting and enjoyable for the participants, but it had been difficult to see any appreciable impact on the business.

It had also been found that expensive strategy documents formulated by consultants could prove impossible to implement because of inadequate management ability.

Common corporate requirements

Each company was hoping to increase the effectiveness of its management, yet it was difficult to see how this might be brought about. The senior and middle managers saw 'little or nothing wrong' with their existing ways of operating. A suggestion that they might improve could quickly create opposition, indignation or other forms of resistance.

Already it was clear that the heads of these four apparently contrasting organizations had two issues in common: how to raise the effectiveness of their management teams, and how to overcome potential internal resistance to any suggestion of a process designed to facilitate this.

In the language developed in this book (see Part 1), these issues equate to the need for a movement between levels. Since the heads of these four organizations achieved the generation of such movement, they merit the title of 'leaders' as defined in Chapter 2!

Common personal requirements

Further questioning revealed that, on an individual level, the four leaders had additional requirements in common. They each wanted their direct reports to think more like they did themselves.

In order to achieve their personal objectives, they needed to see an end to petty rivalry at senior management level - a rivalry which often led to empire-building, resulting in strategically unsatisfactory relationships between departments.

Above all, the four leaders wished to gain greater control over their own time, including the creation of quality planning time. They also wanted to be better at communicating - without knowing exactly what that might mean.

Leading the development process

Along with numerous chief executives and managing directors of companies of contrasting size, age and sector who were facing similar scenarios, these four leaders decided to take the initiative in developing corporate management ability.

This step into the unknown was a truly strategic decision. They did not know what exactly would happen; they only knew that it was both conceptually unrealistic, and characteristic of poor leadership example, to expect the members of their management teams to become more active in their development while they personally remained passive towards their own development.

They also saw that to invest in their own further development may help them to find gains in the elusive areas of time management and communication. This may in turn have an effect on the team of managers below them - if no more than to reduce resistance by setting the example. As a consequence, the development of the whole organization of people below them might be influenced.

But how should they begin, and what should be the subject-matter of study? How could improvements be brought to bear within operating routines that were already long-established?

The first focus of improvement: meetings

Once the decision had been made to invest in their own personal development, the leaders soon began to see where their initial focus should be directed. There was, and is, one area of management life in which communication skills and time management overlap: meetings.

As we saw in Chapter 6, the quality of meetings also offers the interface between the quality of personal influence and the quality of corporate culture. When the head of an organization takes an active personal interest in this aspect of quality, then many aspects of culture may start to change, which sooner or later, will have an impact on both corporate strategy and structure.

As we saw in Chapter 5, it has been estimated that, on

average, managers spend 78 per cent of their time communicating, that is, holding or participating in more or less formal meetings. The remaining 22 per cent of their time is spent preparing for these meetings. When the meetings begin to occupy much more than 78 per cent of time, then the preparation time must be reduced, or the manager must work longer hours. In either event, quality may be lost.

Seeing the truth of this, the four leaders were each keen to participate with others in a personal development programme for chief executives, focused on the quality of meetings. They agreed to devote six days of their time to an intensive study of their current and potential proficiency in the ten archetypal business meetings outlined in Chapter 6.

As well as being gradual, the chief executives agreed that the process could only be made effective by a blend of workshop/seminar work and practical application in the business environment. The purpose of the workshops would be to provide an environment in which the managers' vision could grow.

From seeing more clearly their own starting point and the possibility of developing their thinking and communicating, managers could then design their own aims, objectives and tactics for improvement. This meant that a phased or sequential approach would be needed, with the workshops separated by periods in which new vision could be translated into modified practice based on and supported by a transformed attitude.

Gradual change, through sequential vision workshops

The vision workshops were therefore spread over six months. During the month's interval between each meeting, the participants would try out changes in their personal approach, which they had decided upon during the meeting. This decision would be the result of new insights gained during the seminar. Such insights might be generated by the content of the day or, equally, by the style in which it was managed.

An essential part of the facilitation of strategic development is that an example must always be given of the principles under focus. This places special demands on the content and style of vision workshops.

Decisions for implementation and feedback

The results of the participants' decisions would be reported at the next monthly meeting. This provided a discipline, which helped to break through the potentially subversive influence of habit, personal and corporate, on decisions made at or following the vision workshop.

This had two effects, which the participants themselves had not foreseen. First, they received recognition from their peer group - something which, in the often isolated position of head of organization, had become rare. Second, their rate of learning was increased by the opportunity to hear of the experiments, results, successes, failures and consequent recommendations of their fellow participants.

Changing vision: different applications

As a consequence of their efforts over the period of six months, the four leaders all experienced a development of vision, which resulted in gradual and significant changes in their management and leadership style.

These changes were similar in flavour, because they were all based on the principles of thinking and communicating illustrated in Part 2 of this book. They were different in the detail of application, partly because of differences in (1) starting point, (2) personality and character, and (3) the people environment within the respective businesses.

However, it quickly became clear that few, if any, of the differences in application were related to the fact that the organizations themselves represented different industries, or had different strategic requirements.

All the participants found that, by the end of the six-month period, they had made changes that had an impact at personal, group and corporate levels. First, they had reduced substantially the time required for meetings, while gaining effectiveness in their conduct. This had resulted in greater effectiveness and confidence in the four directions of influence. Similar benefits had been experienced in personal life.

At a team level, each participant now understood much better, through practical experimentation and experience, the nature of group dynamics and motivation. In general, they now saw that they had previously underestimated the potential of some members of their own senior management team, or had not been aware of what was needed to foster their development.

At a corporate level, the four leaders realized that they had all taken the first step towards achieving their different strategic aims.

Like their colleagues through the whole series of chief executive programmes, their experience proved to them beyond all doubt that the first requirement in the generation of continuous organizational improvement is continuous personal research by the head of the organization.

Principles of corporate improvement

As a consequence of their personal experiences, the leaders under discussion each decided to provide a similar personal and team development opportunity for their direct reports. These strategic decisions were based on the process of the development of strategic thinking and decision-making, which had emerged in the course of their own personal development and research.

First, the focus must be on the participants' live issues, beginning with their planning and management of meetings.

Second, they must work in peer groups of (ideally) 6-10 participants in order to generate the best possible team development. Third, the 'drip-feed' or sequential approach - six full-day off-site vision workshops over six months - would be repeated, buttressed in some cases by on-site one-to-one coaching.

Fourth, in addition to the external influence from Mitchell Leadership Consulting , the process must include continuing and visible adaptation by the heads of organization themselves - a continuing example from the top. To facilitate this, four further one-day vision workshops were developed, focused on the subject-matter of Chapter 2 of this book.

In this way the process of creating a strategic, service-oriented culture within organizations of different types was developed in partnership with the client organizations. Altogether, 13 core vision workshops were developed, the last three built around the concepts outlined in Part 1.The structure of the entire process, through which the concepts and practices of strategic decision-making can enter the life of the organization, is illustrated in Figure 7.6.

The fact that the most senior managers take the lead makes it possible for this to be a strategic development process. The natural resistance that may exist at each lower level is overcome, at least in part, by the example that has been set.

As the months go by, and as each level of management begins to understand the underlying principles that unify their apparently different roles and interests, the environment of strategic questioning comes into existence. Gradually, as individual, team and corporate vision grows, the organization itself makes the change from the closed, past-oriented, to the open, goal-oriented cultural level.

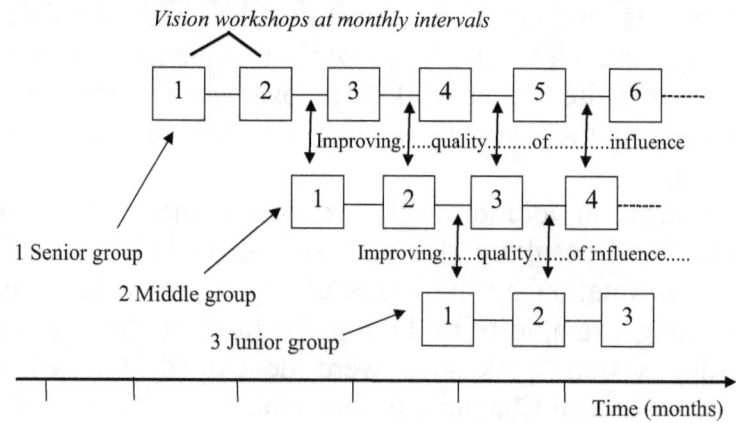

Figure 7.6 Process for the development of a strategic culture.

A cultural habit of strategic questioning

In some organizations, such as Microsoft, these 13 core vision workshops have become an instilled habit of corporate culture to which all current and aspiring managers are exposed - even during periods when all other costs are cut back. Why? Because of the strength given to an organization by the movement between levels of leadership culture.

In the case of Microsoft, both the benefits of the initial decision and the demands that had led to it were deeper and more long-lasting than anticipated. Between 1989 and 1994, the number of employees grew from 60 to 600, and turnover rose from £30 million to £200 million. Over the five-year period, 250 managers were exposed to the strategic process outlined above.

The short-term results included the creation of a common management language, frames of reference for decision-making and the acquisition of high-quality communication skills. In the medium term, appraisal meetings became less judgmental and conducted more towards developing the capability of the human resource; there was increased ability to think and plan strategically throughout the organization, and a recognizable common management style.

Over the long term, a corporate culture emerged which was more flexible, focused on improving and consequently stronger. Of the original management group in 1989, 80 per cent were still with the organization, and growing with it, in 1994. During 1994, Microsoft began a further process: the setting aside of a specified number of days per quarter in which Mitchell Leadership Consulting was commissioned to foster the growth of a new generation of strategic questions.

Security in strategic, structural and cultural change

Shandon Scientific, the subsidiary of Life Sciences International, experienced different kinds of change. The number of employees in 1989 was 230. By 1994 this had grown to 260, and two levels of management had been stripped away. Revenue in the period had grown from £10 million to £40 million, and all profitability targets had been met. During this period 60 managers, including the managing director and board, followed the development path outlined in general above.

From the company's point of view, the benefits could again be divided into short, medium and long term. In the short term, management was equipped to manage rapid change, encompassing a move from traditional manufacturing to state-of-the-art practices. Product lines were rationalized, manufacturing costs were reduced and cell manufacturing established.

A series of study groups for middle management, run by senior management, helped to free Shandon from the secrecy and defensiveness of the previous management. A company-wide appraisal process was introduced, and improved communication channels accompanied a development in decision-making ability.

In the medium term, the principles and practices of the third level of leadership gave the company a greater ability to integrate acquisitions rapidly and effectively into the corporate culture.

This, accompanied by a greater awareness of the demands and implications of higher quality recruitment, strengthened Shandon's market position. By 1994, Shandon had a 50 per cent share of the UK market and 25 per cent of the US and European markets.

In the longer term, cooperation has replaced internal competition, and managers who were previously afraid to make decisions now accept their responsibility and authority so that decision-making is faster and more efficient. The company has become a market-driven organization as managers' awareness of and responsiveness to customer needs have been enhanced. As a result, customer services and relations have improved, and new product development opportunities have been identified.

The level of management thinking has been raised. The company is now clearly focused on where it is going and how it is going to get there. Shandon is well positioned to expand through the introduction of new products and further acquisitions. Labour turnover is down from 10 to 6 per cent, and absenteeism has fallen dramatically since the exposure of managers to the principles of strategic decision-making.

Smooth mergers and acquisitions

Glynwed Metal Services adopted a similar approach. The initial benefit was the generation of a way of communicating which motivated and acted as a binding agent for the geographically spread group of companies. Managers who were previously fire-fighting on a daily basis learned to prepare, plan and manage their business much more effectively. A new confidence allowed them to address and resolve problems rather than avoid them, particularly where staff were concerned.

As communication and trust improved, managers learned to ask for, listen to and act on the views of their staff. Teamwork both within and across the companies improved dramatically. These cultural improvements strengthened the ability of the company to merge several of its branches during and after the recession, with minimal impact on the customer base.

In 1993-4, the acquisition of the RTZ Metals business was accomplished smoothly and highly profitably, despite doubts expressed by accountants prior to the purchase. During 1994 the definition and implementation of strategy developed further, as will be discussed in Chapter 8.

Strength through the recession

STA Travel's strategic development initiative helped not only to achieve the initial requirements mentioned above but also to gain strength and market share during the testing period of the recession, which forced several of their competitors out of business.

In the early 1990s, following the promotion of the UK managing director to the role of chief executive, STA Travel's work with Mitchell Leadership Consulting spread from the UK to become a worldwide initiative fostering the growth of a global management culture, based on a high level of professionalism and interchangeability.

Within a shallow management structure, managers have a clear sense of purpose and a clear understanding of their responsibility and authority. The shared management language has improved communication both vertically and horizontally within the management structure.

A process for internal growth

Successful organizations continue to grow. As maturity increases, the agenda for growth can change. The visible structural and external changes give way to a focus on internal growth and development, the effects of which become more subtly visible over time.

Internal growth can be seen as a progression between the closed, open and strategic levels of leadership culture. Through this progression, the organization is slowly released from its past and is oriented first towards new goals and results and then gradually towards an ethic in which leadership and service become identical.

Possibilities for the process through which such growth can be generated are illustrated by the case histories outlined above.

Alternatives are possible, in which work on strategic thinking precedes the focus on decision-making and communication. Whatever the order, the approach must be such that a growth of vision brings about a development in attitude towards leadership and responsibility, which becomes visible in conduct.

This elusive quality of organizational growth requires a parallel growth in teamwork, which in turn demands the personal development of team members. By working simultaneously on personal and team growth for teams throughout the organization, the organization's internal growth is developed.

We have seen four principles on which the process of growth is based: work on strengths as well as weaknesses; imitate the natural learning process; a unique development process for each executive; use the live issues. The process is similar for all organizations, the only differences lie in the starting point and in the precise detail of implementation. Similar differences have been seen to exist between teams and individuals within each organization.

The process is cumulative in its effect, culminating in the creation of the most valuable form of competitive advantage: a strategic organization, built on a service mentality both internally and externally.

CHAPTER 8

Building the strategic organization

From the past, to the future, to the present

We can see the internal growth of organizations as a progression of orientation from the past to the future to the present. A focus on precedent gives way first to an emphasis on the achieving of goals.

In time this may develop further to a greater feeling for responsibility now, bringing a relative freedom from projection forwards or backwards in time.

Such a progression must be generated by a parallel growth in teamwork, from static to dynamic to organic. This in turn demands a corresponding personal development among team members, from passive to active to visionary.

Generically, we have defined these levels of leadership as closed, open and strategic. Closed leadership and closed teamwork mean a closed organization. Open leadership and open teamwork mean an open organization. Strategic leadership and strategic teamwork mean a strategic organization.

Strategic leaders, teams and organizations share a similar understanding of their context. In Chapter 1 we explored the four primary relationships in a manager's authority: upwards, downwards, sideways within the organization and sideways

211

outside the organization.

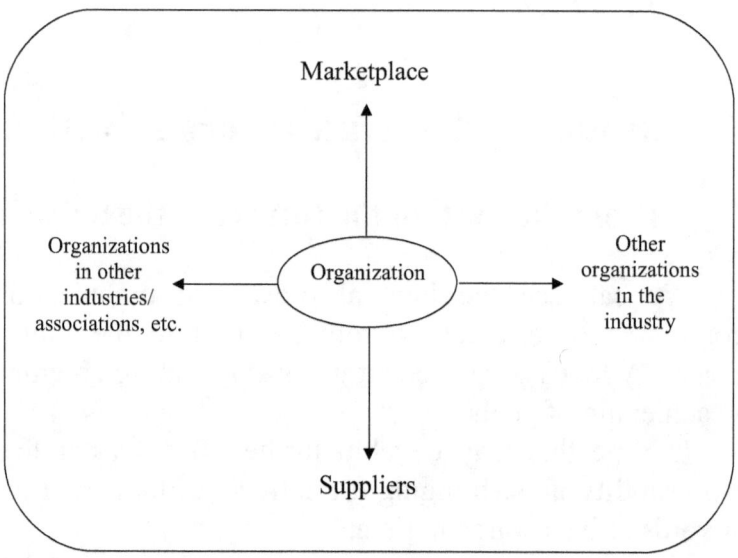

Figure 8.1 The context of the strategic organization.

Strategic organizations and teams understand their contexts similarly as one of four primary relationships based on authority. While the occupants of these four positions of relative authority may vary from organization to organization and team to team, the essential strategic contexts for organizations and teams are those illustrated in Figures 8.1 and 8.2. The Principle of Strategic Responsibility (see Figure 8.3) applies and is felt accordingly.

Leadership Development

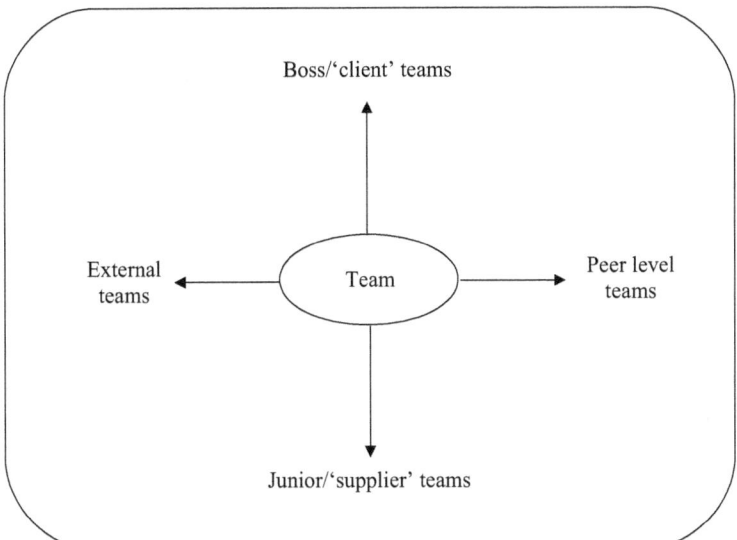

Above: Figure 8.2 The context of the strategic team.
Below: Figure 8.3 The Principle of Strategic Responsibility.

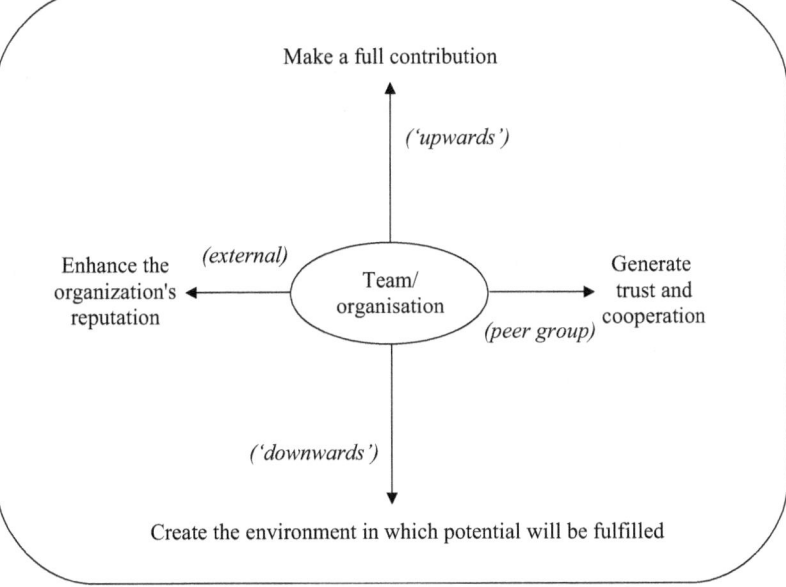

Interesting and stimulating questions may arise from the integration of the Principle of Strategic Responsibility with the strategic contexts of organizations and teams. For example, it is immediately obvious that the strategic organization will feel a responsibility to create an environment in which suppliers will fulfill their potential and thus make a full contribution.

By focusing on the implications of the responsibility 'upwards', teams can begin to develop the level of in-company service that is characteristic of the strategic organization. New light may also be thrown on popular ideas about competition through price and differentiation by examining the position of competitors in the context of the organization's strategic responsibilities.

The place of shareholders

It may be asked why shareholders are not shown at the higher level of authority in an organization. From the point of view of the strategic context of the organization, the shareholders are considered to be part of the organization, as 'stakeholders', similar to managers and staff.

The context in which shareholders occupy a position of higher authority is generally only within the strategic context of the board or chairman.

The next context 'up' can be particularly interesting, for it shows the 'downwards' responsibility of shareholders as to create the environment in which the board can fulfill its potential. And what is the responsibility 'upwards' of shareholders?

The organization's strategic role definition

In Chapter 5 we explored ways in which a strategic role definition can be developed for an individual, and the advantages that can arise in terms of flexibility, focus, motivation and the generation of opportunities for recognition.

Similar possibilities exist for organizations and teams. The development of strategic role definitions and statements in these contexts indicate the degree of growth of vision.

By way of example, we shall study the strategy statements developed and issued by Glynwed Metals Services (GMS) between 1992 and 1994.

External signs of the growth of vision

GMS's initial use of Mitchell Leadership Consulting , indicated in the previous chapter, signaled the company's gradual transition from a relatively closed to a relatively open leadership culture.

This was reflected in the organization's increased ability to create and implement structural and strategic changes. These included the merging of some of its own branches, the curtailing of its US activities and the simultaneous expansion of its European interests.

Through an increased ability to respond to market conditions and to find quick and substantial cost savings, GMS was able to maintain a strong position through the recession years.

This transition was accompanied by the formulation and publication of statements of corporate vision and mission. Also published internally were corporate strategic aims derived from and relating to the statements. This initial formulation of strategy, reproduced in Example 8.1, illustrates a definite phase in the organization's development.

Example 8.1
Glynwed Metal Services : 1992 strategy statements

VISION

In the United Kingdom there exists and will continue to exist a requirement for a link between the user and the manufacturer of high-value metals. Our aim is to be the first choice provider of this service.

MISSION

Our purpose is to anticipate, influence and satisfy the needs of our customers. This will be achieved by dedicated and competent employees maintaining high standards of quality and service, whilst attaining predetermined financial objectives.

STRATEGIC AIMS

People

We believe people are the company's key resource.

♦ To employ high calibre people who are committed to our values.

♦ To provide an environment where all employees can achieve their full potential.

♦ To share information through effective communications.

Sales and marketing

It is accepted that success will be achieved through being a marketing led company.

♦ To be the customers' first choice supplier of our products and services by providing a competitive, reliable and responsive service that reflects and meets their continual changing needs.

♦ To retain market leadership by being the largest multi-metal distributor.

♦ To remain the largest independent distributor of each core product. In market share terms, this means first or close second.

♦ To manage and further develop our brands to offer our customers a real choice in satisfying their needs.

♦ To develop long-term partnerships with customers with a view to reducing total procurement costs. This will be achieved through investment in technology and people.

Standards, procedures and systems

We recognize that quality has become a primary buyer value.

♦ To operate quality systems in line with internationally recognized standards.

♦ To ensure product quality and documentation continually meets or exceeds customer requirements.

♦ To continue to exploit computer technology as a source of competitive advantage.

Suppliers

We acknowledge that, as an Independent, the forging of strategic partnerships is of fundamental importance to our business.

♦ To develop long-term relationships with selected suppliers that share our values.

Finance

We believe financial performance is critical to the ongoing prosperity of shareholders and staff.
♦ To meet or exceed predetermined financial objectives. This would include profit, ROA and cash flow.

During 1994 GMS implemented further significant structural and cultural changes. What had effectively been two executive boards became one, and the earlier strategy statements were replaced with those shown in Example 8.2. A comparison of the key elements of these two sets of strategy statements can throw light on the nature of the transformation between the open and strategic levels of leadership.

The first set (Example 8.1) was a significant step at the time of its introduction. Against a background of board meetings and senior management thinking which still focused largely on the mechanics of the business - such as stock controls, pricing, financial targets and branch performance - it opened the way to the gradual refocusing of management thinking on an expanded agenda.

At the same time, it contained elements that also brought about a closer focus on detail, which led to quality improvements throughout the branch structure.

An educative process

The first set of statements played an important part in the organization's management education, by creating a framework of policy in relation to larger issues. Through the process of its creation, as much as through subsequent reference to it, the senior management levels expanded their own vision.

The limitation on this first set, and the aspect that keeps it firmly in the realm of open rather than strategic leadership, is that it cannot be easily and directly integrated with daily executive activity.

The second set of strategic statements, issued during 1994, took the development process a stage further and established the framework for the transition to strategic leadership. The vision statement was simplified, now including the international aspect of the business and omitting the aim/objective element of the earlier version (see Example 8.2).

The new formulation of the mission stated more clearly the contribution of the company within its marketplace, with less reference to the manner in which this would be achieved. The new, simplified wording also made it more meaningful and more easily remembered. Above all, these revised statements could be used in the planning process.

Example 8.2
Glynwed Metal Services : 1994 strategy statements

VISION
UK and international users and manufacturers of high-value metals will continue to benefit from the quality of distribution which GMS provides.

MISSION
Be a permanent link between users and manufacturers of high-value metals.

STRATEGIC AIMS
Customers - Develop long-term relationships with customers
Marketing - Create easily recognisable value

Product - Anticipate, influence and meet changes in demand
Suppliers - Create the conditions in which suppliers can excel
People - Attract, develop and retain people who will serve the Mission
Distribution - Create and develop a reputation for excellence
Growth - Continuously identify and develop new business opportunities to serve the Mission.

Simplification and integration

In the revised version, seven strategic aims replaced the 18 previous elements, and were formulated in a way that was less likely to draw attention to the organization's view of its own inadequacies.

The new aims also provided the focus for the members of the restructured board to design their own role definitions. The main aim was that the newly formulated role definitions, taken together, should create confidence that the corporate strategic aims were being fully served by the board.

The board members each accepted the corporate mission statement as a personal vision. They then formulated statements of purpose for their own jobs. From these, each then developed strategic aims and, later, objectives for each aim. Once these were in place, the process could be repeated at the next level of management, and so on down the organization.

Three layers of awareness

A very important aspect to emerge from this process was the fact that, as we saw in Chapter 1, strategic decision-making requires an awareness of, and participation by each individual in, three distinct layers of strategy.

All the people involved need to know where their own strategies, or role definitions, fit both within that of their boss and that of their direct reports. This in itself gives a further indication of why the development of the strategic organization has to evolve from a top-down initiative.

Values and quality now built-in

Through this process of strategic formulation that is characteristic of strategic leadership, an important aspect can be seen which impacts strongly on questions of quality and corporate values.

Until the formulation of the second set of strategic statements, there had been much discussion among senior managers at GMS about quality and values.

Once the revised strategic aims were in place and linked to job definitions, it was clear that both quality and values were now becoming built into the cultural and strategic fabric of the organization. There was no longer any need to regard quality and values as something separate from management and leadership practice.

Towards a service-oriented (= strategic) leadership culture

The case histories outlined above and in Chapter 7 point the way to a methodology for leading the organization towards a quality of internal action, or culture, which is based on an attitude of service.

While the application of this methodology will vary between and even within different organizations, its essence is universal. This is illustrated in Figure 8.4.

In the service-oriented culture - the culture of the third level of leadership (as defined in Chapter 2) - a balance is achieved and maintained between vision and action, both horizontally and vertically within the organization. In such a culture, the understanding, development and sustenance of this balance becomes the central concern of leadership.

The balance between vision and action is indicated in Figure 8.4. by the diagonal line which represents strategic decision-making (as defined in Chapter 2). As we have seen, strategic decision-making is characteristic only of the third level of leadership. In respectively greater and lesser proportions, the second and first levels of leadership feature in decision-making which we have defined in Chapter 2 as open, closed and automatic.

Leadership Development

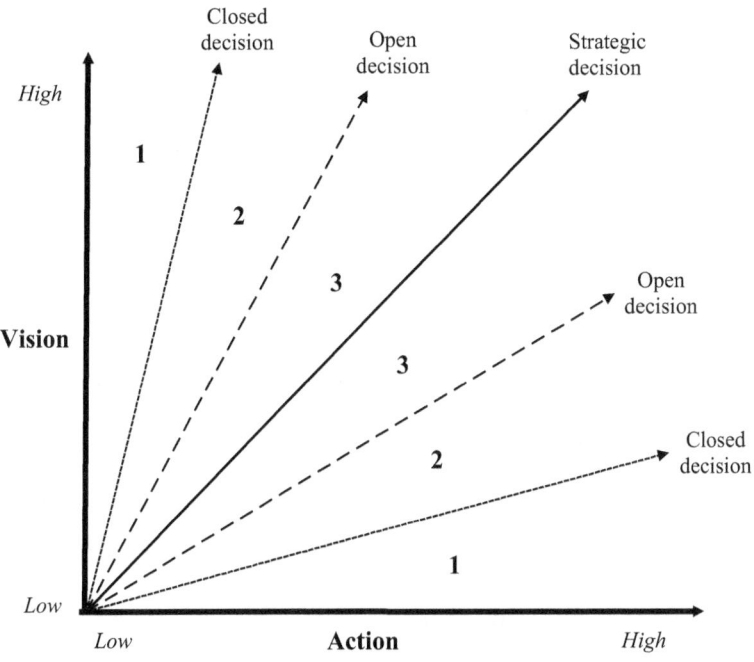

Figure 8.4 Moving from a closed to an open leadership culture.

In a Level 1 culture, for example, vision is not consciously related to action. It may be that vision exists only in the form of unspoken assumptions. Alternatively, vision may be well articulated at senior levels, but the quality of decision-making, communication and consequent influence fails to generate the corresponding action in other parts of the organization. This does not mean that people are not working hard!

The Level 2 culture features a more fully articulated vision, linked more effectively to action. Its development can be brought about through initiatives of the type indicated in Chapter 7. Whether it can then be sustained will depend largely on the quality of subsequent leadership within the organization.

Generally speaking, the long-term usefulness of any externally sourced influence on the culture of an organization is in direct proportion to its contribution to a movement towards the quality of decision-making represented by the solid diagonal line in Figure 8.4. When such a quality of decision-making has been developed and is characteristic of the organization's internal action, then a service-oriented culture exists.

The prevention of organizational decay

Those who have already championed the progression towards the third level of leadership and management in their own organizations are keen to help others make similar decisions.

Aware of the impossibility of communicating their vision directly, they have turned to a long-proven means of stimulating the understanding of others: the story.

To help the nature of movement between levels to become more visible, it may be useful to include a story developed in the course of a series of senior management seminars which focused on strategic decision-making.

The story highlights the subtle tendencies that can usher in decay even - perhaps especially - in the most firmly established organizations. It indicates in broad principle the kind of strategic focus needed to maintain growth and prevent such decay.

THE LEGEND OF THE OCTOPUS

There once lived an Octopus, with an Eye fixed on the future and a Mind forever focused on the question: *'What am I for, and how should I live?'*

With such an Eye and Mind, steady forward motion was easy through the enthusiastic support of its eight legs which the Octopus called, collectively, the FIRM CAPS---a name derived from their vital functions: Finance, Image, Research and development, Marketing, Customer service, Administration, Production and Sales.

Whenever something new appeared on the horizon, the Octopus immediately carried through a 5-point plan which was inherent in its nature:

- A message would pass from the Eye of the Octopus to one or more of the FIRM CAPS, giving information on what had happened and requesting an appropriate response.
- The FIRM CAPS would agree on one or more proposal(s), to be presented to the Mind for a final decision.
- The Mind would decide new actions required, taking into account the data from the Eye and the idea of the FIRM CAPS.
- The FIRM CAPS member who had originated the approved proposal would take the first step forward--- and the other FIRM CAPS members would show their support by quickly following---neatly adjusting their own footwork.
- As the Mind concentrated again on the future, it would

send a message of congratulation to the FIRM CAPS---particularly to innovative members.

In this way, progress was steady and orderly. The path to the horizon was always clear, and such was the harmony between Eye, Mind and FIRM CAPS that much of what lay beyond the horizon was accurately anticipated.

The Octopus became known far and wide as a model of efficiency and effectiveness. Other Octopuses copied its style, and its offspring did so instinctively. Soon FIRM CAPS everywhere enjoyed, understood and took pride in their role of securing and adding value to their own organism.

Then one day, something happened. Nobody knows quite when or how.

Some say that Sales insulted Customer service, or that Production grew jealous of Marketing; others insisted that Research and development became irritable towards Admin., or even that Finance wanted to kill Image. Later rumors suggested that at least one of the FIRM CAPS thought it knew better than the Eye how to see, or better than the Mind how to decide.

Whatever the cause, the Mind was forced to stop making decisions about the future in order to attend to the FIRM CAPS, which had started tripping each other up and whose proposals were becoming unreliable. In the tangle that followed, the Octopus turned around several times, so that the Eye could no longer be sure of the direction in which the future lay. To escape the trauma, the Eye became reclusive, closed, and sang itself to sleep with a lullaby: 'I am an Eye---how happy I am! The FIRM CAPS may argue as much as they can!'

The Mind was so busy trying to find out what was going on that the FIRM CAPS realized that they actually *could* now see better than the Eye, which was asleep, and they could now make better decisions than the Mind, which could now make none. So, rejoicing in their new 'freedom', the eight legs had what was destined to be the last meeting they ever held that produced deliberate action.

The outcome of the meeting was that the FIRM CAPS resolved to re-organize themselves under the banner of a new 'corporate philosophy' called F-CARPISM. This 'new philosophy' had four central tenets:

- As founder-members of F-CARPISM, we have a right to be busy.
- As long as we are busy, what we are doing must be important.
- As long as what we are doing is important according to the above definition, we needn't do anything else (this includes looking pleased about anything, or making improvements).
- We shall set up a new department, called MIFS? . . . CRAP!!, to take responsibility for the quality of movement and future development of octopus legs. To save our time, it must be a self-contained unit in which existing legs need not be involved.

Some time later, a fifth tenet was added at a meeting where all the former FIRM CAPS were represented by proxy. They agreed, 'in absentia', that:

- It seems to be working fine under the first four tenets, so no others will ever be necessary.

The Mind of the Octopus, meanwhile, tired of trying to disentangle the legs, became absorbed in the study of the art of cutting Octopus' toenails. One day, as part of this study, the Mind invited an Octopologist for lunch. The Octopologist, who was an expert on Octopus welfare, carried a large box, with a lid made out of a mirror.

Hearing that the first step in taking an interest in Octopology was to look into the mirror, the Mind was compelled to rouse the Eye, which stared into it in disbelief. All this time, the Octopus had had its back to the future; its legs were completely intertwined and, as far as the Eye could see, Sharks were gathering in the background.

The Octopologist asked: 'As an Octopus, what are you for, and how do you live and grow?' The Mind was dumbfounded.

The Octopologist continued: 'First we need to find an answer to these questions and, at the same time, escape from the Sharks. Here is a plan which will enable you to do this: it involves a compass, a map and four sets of crutches. The real challenge will be to re-establish a group of FIRM CAPS to counter the past and present impact of F-CARPISM.

'When this has been achieved', the Octopologist added, 'it will also be necessary for you as an Octopus to build into your own system a protection mechanism against any future influence of F-CARPISM which will at the same time secure your whole organism in both this and any future environment. For this to happen, every part of your organism must learn both to serve its current purpose and to allow itself to be prepared for future purposes.'

The Mind thought this was a great plan. So did the Eye, for a while. Then, being accustomed to sleep, it closed itself and began to have nightmares about Sharks.

Unsure now, the Mind turned to the Octopologist and said: 'It was good of you to come; leave this with me, and I'll get back to you just as soon as I've okayed your plan with the members of F-CARPISM and the MIFS? . . . CRAP!! department. . . . '

At the start of the story, the organism or organization represented by the octopus moves, operates and reproduces itself efficiently and effectively within its environment. It is able to anticipate external changes and to adapt quickly through smooth internal practices.

The beginnings of decay are unseen, and become the subject of gossip and recrimination only in retrospect. The focus on the environment falters, individual egos and politicking take the place of collective awareness and service, and the culture slides towards apathy and negativity.

The invention of the MIFS? . . . CRAP!!' department was intended by the managers behind the writing of this story to represent the emergence of the personnel function. More specifically, they felt that while such a function has a supportive role to play, it is too often given the responsibility, without the authority, for management training and development at senior level. As a consequence, there may be no advanced training or development work at senior level, because the personnel function cannot influence strategic decisions on it.

The Mind, representing a chief executive, becomes sidetracked until a chance meeting with the 'Octopologist' creates the possibility for a strategic decision, which, if taken, would reverse the process of decay. The Eye opens, creating almost enough vision for the decision to be made. But at the critical instant, fear takes over, and the Mind decides to avoid the decision. It will be checked with those whose very attitude constitutes the problem that the decision itself would eventually remedy. Therefore the decision cannot, and will not, be made.

Chief executives' attitudes towards leadership

The senior managers behind the creation of this story were personally familiar with the real-life business situation represented by the dilemma confronting the Mind.

Without feeling particularly dissatisfied with their management teams, they sensed that some improvement might be possible that would strengthen the organization in its environment. They made the decision, and *took the first step themselves…*